CHILD OF THE ISLE

CROWVUS

Copyright © 2018 by Susan Crow

All rights reserved. This book or any portion thereof may not be reproduced or used in any manner whatsoever without the express written permission of the publisher except for the use of brief quotations in a book review.

First Published in 2018

Crowvus, 53 Argyle Square, Wick, KW1 5AJ

Copyright © Text Susan Crow 2018

Copyright © Cover Image Crowvus 2018

ISBN 978-0-9957860-4-2

www.crowvus.com

THE ISLAND TOWNSHIP

Circling, adjusting his sleep position,
An old dog moves in the pale summer dust.
Watch his ancestors through ashes of years,
Where religious freedom grew on the farm
On rising ground in the island township.
Roger de Mowbray haunts the fine Vine Garth
With hunting cur, leggy and rough coated,
While street dogs steal from sellers in their yards.
Climbing beams of time where the Dutch, with hounds,
Engineer success, depriving farmers'
Families of promised use of waste lands.
The farmyard barks with curses old and new.
Then a different growl, reviving faith,
Came within this spectrum, prismatic hope;
All talk of Wesley in the Churchyard
In Epworth where communions are made
With God, and thanks given for history.

Beginnings

When I started building our family tree, I soon became an addict. Should never have experimented - or should I? Apart from my father's maternal grandfather, I have seen photos of all of my great-grandparents, which has proved to be of significance when I enter the almost-fantasy world of my ancestors. I research them well, aiming for accuracy - double-checking each morsel of information. I imagine their joys, their pain and their setting - where they lived, how they got around and what their daily patterns were. I love them with an affection which bridges the gap between then and now.

So I thought I might write their stories - might do more general historical research and present the world with biographical accounts of my predecessors. Then I stopped that thought process and admitted to myself that there would be too much conjecture, too much assumption, too many guesses, and an enormous amount of me! Who would want to read about me? Well, I suppose nobody would. There is nothing significant about me. Really nothing special at all. However, there may be something of interest in the places, the people and the times which were my personal history. I remember a post-war pure world of beauty and hope, a world of simplicity, sunshine in Summer, snow in Winter, and the thrill of learning more and more each day. It was a world of thankfulness. The war - which was never supposed to have happened, given that the Great War of 1914-1918 was "the war to end all wars" - was over.

I will write down some snippets of Susanalia and try my very best to be honest in my accounts, but please allow for memory lapses and for the corruption of time. I mean to do good things. Please forgive my failures.

The first six months or so were spent in a tiny dwelling down Belshaw Lane in Belton. It was attached to a bigger house and very basic. My mother has spoken of black-leading the range and once mentioned the elderly man who lived in the bigger house. Our cottage was close to my paternal grandparents' house, Rose Cottage, and at the far end of the small community known as Carrhouse, sometimes Carhouse. Our end of Belton was an old-fashioned community, quite apart from the rest of the village. Across the road from that first home there was a secluded house belonging to Jack Needham. Jack was a recluse but lived close by his brother, Fred, and sister-in-law, Eva (formerly Addlesee). Other close neighbours included well-known local names such as Burgess, Fox, Hackney, Kitson and Walls.

If you were to walk the length of Belshaw Lane and pass "Hilltop" on your left and the pond on your right, go over the route of the old railway and continue along the sandy track, you will, in dry weather, get a shoe full of dust and eventually come out on the road which joins Epworth and Sandtoft. After years of living in Scotland, I smile now when I remember my granny saying "Shall we go for a walk up on Hilltop, Susie?" It really wasn't a very lofty height! I am awestruck by the majesty of our Highland mountains, but the peaceful Lincolnshire countryside and the wonderful big skies still call to me.

Mum thought Belshaw Lane was the back and beyond and, thirteen years later, when Dad and Mum built their bungalow on the clover field adjacent to Mrs. Franks' house, she was firm in her resolve to have transport provided for shopping. Mum is not a driver herself. She tells the story of Dad trying to teach her to drive on the aerodrome at Sandtoft and how, in spite of the vast open space, she managed to back into a hangar - with a bump.

We moved from Belton to Battlegreen, Epworth when I was about six months old. Battlegreen, or Battle Green, is believed to have been the site of a battle between the people of the Isle of Axholme and Vermuyden's countrymen when the Dutch took great swathes of the Isle as payment for their drainage of this northernmost Lincolnshire fenland. Back in the seventeenth century their efforts were unwelcome and threatened the livelihoods of many Islonians.

The house in Battlegreen was very old and likely to have been influenced by the architectural style of the Dutch, with its steep gable ends. Like my first home, it has been demolished. At that time my father worked as a potato salesman and my mother was a full-time wife and mother. I have the idea that the first floor of our house was accessed by a sturdy ladder, but I am unsure why I think that as my memories begin at our next address. I do remember, however, walking past the house when I was a little bit older and being intrigued by its character and age. The bricks were very old and had, at one time, been given a coat of paint.

It wasn't a large house, and when my brother, who was born there, was a babe in arms, our family moved to a bigger cottage, just a little way along Battlegreen, up the non-metalled track towards Burnham Beck. Studcross Cottage was our home for about seven years. It is still there but looks very different now - hemmed in by modern housing. Dear draughty, humble and homely Studcross Cottage was where my earliest memories began.

We don't use punts anymore

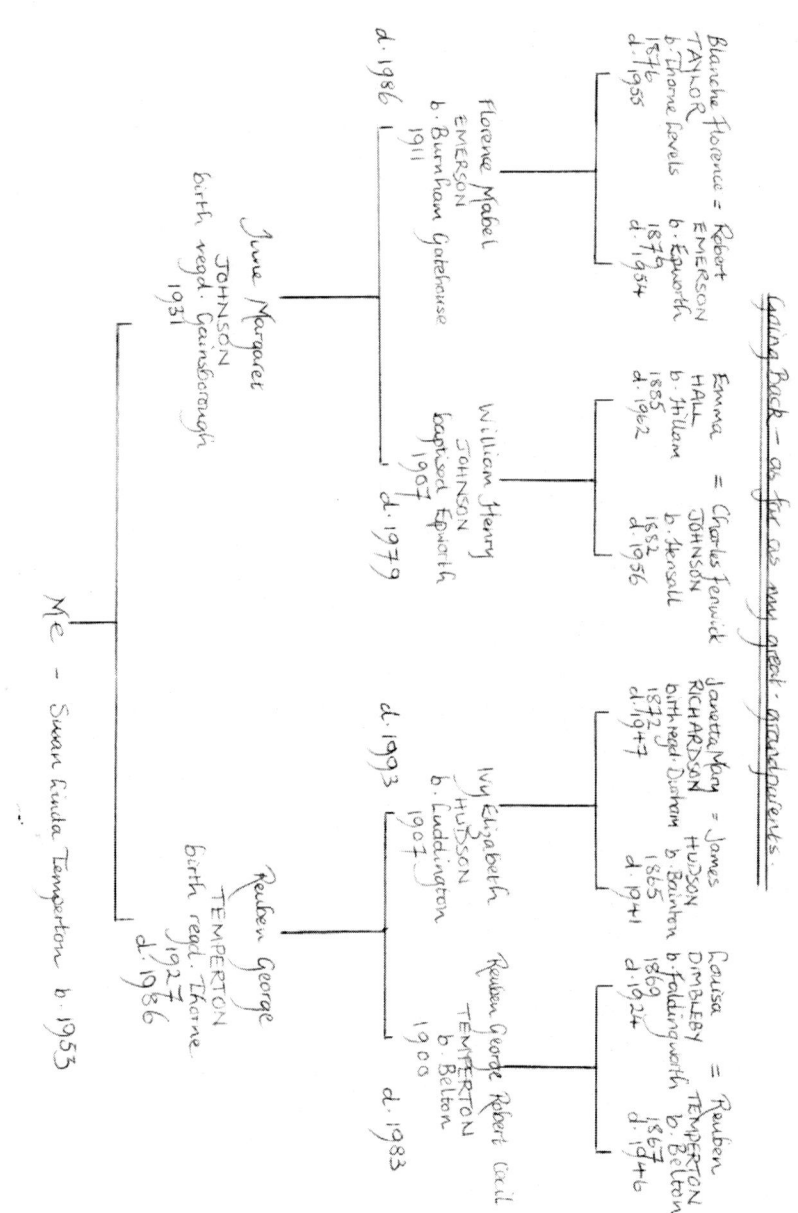

Going Back – as far as my great-grandparents.

Blanche Florence TAYLOR
b. Thorne Levels 1876
d. 1955
= Robert EMERSON
b. Epworth 1879
d. 1954

Emma HALL
b. Hillam 1855
d. 1962
= Charles Fenwick JOHNSON
b. Hensall 1852
d. 1936

Janetta Mary RICHARDSON
birth regd. Durham 1872
d. 1947
= James HUDSON
b. Barmston 1865
d. 1941

Louisa DIMBLEBY
b. Foldingworth 1869
d. 1924
= Reuben TEMPERTON
b. Belton 1867
d. 1946

Florence Mabel EMERSON
b. Burnham Gatehouse 1911
d. 1986

William Henry JOHNSON
baptised Epworth 1907
d. 1979

Ivy Elizabeth HUDSON
b. Luddington 1907
d. 1993

Reuben George Robert Cecil TEMPERTON
b. Belton 1900
d. 1983

June Margaret JOHNSON
birth regd. Gainsborough 1931

Reuben George TEMPERTON
birth regd. Thorne 1927
d. 1986

Me — Susan Linda Temperton b. 1953

Going Back

In November 2015 we took Mum to Studcross. She looked and looked again. It was a while before she was able to see the cottage we lived in - although we were parked across the road. Studcross Cottage itself has been modernised - show me a Lincolnshire cottage which hasn't! [I'm wandering a bit here but I will share this with you - there used to be an old farmhouse at Churchtown, Belton. We knew it as Bell's Farm. I pedalled past it each day and promised myself that I would buy it and make it my own. Instead, I picked up my bike at Mrs. Shapland's shop, after getting off the school bus one day, started for home and I never quite got over what I saw. It was being pulled apart. Bell's Farm was destroyed. A while later, a Regency style house was built there.]

Back to Studcross Cottage and its altered appearance. It wasn't the changes which had been made to the house which so confused Mum - it was the number of buildings which had gone up around it and, instead of the dirt track which served for our lane in the 50s and early 60s, there was a surfaced road. When I was a child, I wore kilts or pinafore dresses in the winter months with knee socks held up by homemade elastic garters. This meant that there was no protection for my knees when I stumbled - and I did. When the crests of the ruts in the lane were frozen they were sharp as knives. In summer, clouds of dust swirled around any vehicle which was driven past our house, slowly settling as the engine sound died away. We rode push bikes at our peril. The unevenness was hazardous. Mike, my brother, spent some time with his leg in plaster after an accident at The Thurlow. Mum had to wheel him around in an old pushchair for a while - not too bad on tarmac - but not at all easy in the lane.

In those days, across the lane from Studcross Cottage, there was a field. I remember vegetables being harvested there and sometimes wheat or oats. My birthday is in June and, one year, my little friends and I took my party across the lane and into the wheat field. There were so many poppies growing amongst the wheat that we stained our party frocks with poppy juice - as well as being a nuisance to the farmer. Mum wasn't pleased and doubtless the other mums were none too happy either. Who would have thought that poppies were capable of such staining?

The far end of that field was edged by the railway embankment - the Axholme Joint Railway used to run along there. The passenger trains ended in 1933, long before the goods trains, and - towards the end of the railway's existence - the track was used as a siding. It was 1965 when goods trains ceased to run on the Axholme Joint. Mum's family, on both sides, were railway people. When I was small, my Grandma Johnson decided that I should experience a railway journey so she took me, by train, to the cinema in Scunthorpe by way of Keadby-with-Althorpe Station. We went to see Lady and the Tramp. I loved the whole experience. It was also important for Grandma to share her railway history a little with me as her father and brothers had worked for the railway and she herself had operated the level crossing gate on Jeffrey Lane in Belton. (Great-Grandad Emerson had been a plate layer on the railways in France during World War 1.) When Grandma and Grandad Johnson had moved from Haxey in 1940, they went to the gatehouse on Jeffrey Lane and there they brought up their three children through the war years - when they also had Grandma's niece from Manchester to stay for safety - and beyond. Grandad Johnson's family were also very much involved in the railways. Great-Grandad Charles Fenwick Johnson was Station Master at Haxey and his death in 1956 was mourned by many Islonians.

When Mike and I went up toay by Burnham Beck, we looked for chicken chalk but also for the ghosts of our great-grandparents, Robert and Blanche Emerson. They had lived there with our grandma and our great-uncles, at Burnham Gatehouse, before moving to Station Road in Epworth. Robert and Blanche died when I was very small. It was easy to imagine that we could hear other childish voices there - from long ago. Grandma Johnson (née Emerson) used to speak of walking along the railway with her brothers on their way to school. They went to the same school as we did - Epworth County Primary, Battlegreen. It has been a restaurant for some time but I remember its classrooms fragranced with hyacinths in the springtime and decked with our handmade paper chains and Chinese lanterns for Christmas. I remember autumn leaves strewn over the nature table and the wonderful coolness of the cloakrooms when we were marched indoors after a hot summer's playtime.

Years later, I told the children I taught that they should love going to school but that they should love home more - I did. I wonder why some of us love home and everything associated with it and others can't wait for the next outing or holiday. Myself, I enjoy my holidays very much but I always feel a little sad when the front door has closed behind me as we set off on our travels and, when the day of departure for home arrives, I am ready and homeward bound with enthusiasm. "Mid pleasures and palaces, Though we may roam, Be it ever so humble, There's no place like home."

My earliest memory is of being allowed to eat a Duncan's Walnut Whip in our "best room" one Boxing Day. I was very small but felt quite grown-up as Mr. Duncan made his Walnut Whips for adults! They are no longer Duncan's and I don't think you can buy the maple or coffee flavours anymore but they are still available with vanilla in the middle. Chocolate was such a treat. It was really meant for Easter and Christmas. At Christmas our neighbours and the neighbours of my Granny Ivy and Grandad Bobby Temperton would give us a present of chocolate or special biscuits. Mrs. Burgess, Mr. and Mrs. Needham and Mr. and Mrs. Kitson from Belshaw Lane, and Mr. and Mrs. Gravel from Studcross gave us pretty little tins of biscuits, Toblerones, Nestle's chocolate pennies and other treats at Christmas. To us, these were absolutely delightful. We had respect for our neighbours and I think of them with gratitude - not for the chocolate but for their patient kindness and interest.

Perhaps the nature of neighbourliness has changed since then - I think it has - but there is still an awareness that we cannot exist without some interaction with those around us. Jack and Joan Pilsworth sold greengroceries at the point where Studcross Lane left Battlegreen. We called them Uncle Jack and Auntie Joan. You simply didn't address adults by their Christian names in those days. It was either Mr. and Mrs. Pilsworth or Uncle Jack and Auntie Joan. Alongside their property a path linked Battlegreen with Fieldside. At the other side, and between their house and ours, was a field in which I remember Frank Johnson growing sugar beet. When we were at Primary School, Frank's daughter, Pauline, and I were friends. They lived at Ellers Tavern. It was down West End but the area known as Ellers went as far as Northferry Lane, which linked with Belshaw Lane, Belton, where my grandparents lived.

Apart from Mrs. Belcher's house on the corner, the only buildings on the opposite side of the lane from us were four red brick homes, Myers Villas, standing between the lane and the railway embankment. At the end lived a man who rode his bike with a sack slung over his shoulder. In the sack were rabbits. He seemed very pleasant but my little self could never forgive him for the rabbits! Next to him lived the Dawson

Family - each a colourful character - and next to them lived a girl called Zena and her two brothers. In the house on the roadside lived the Gravel Family - so kind, all of them. Mrs. Gravel was a very clever needlewoman and Mr. Gravel kept birds in an aviary. He and his son, Cliffy, were expert gardeners and built a wishing well in their garden. Cliffy always did well at Epworth Show with his produce and miniature gardens.

If you passed our house and turned left, you came to the mere. By the side of the mere lived Billy Taylor, someone else who went about on his bicycle. Mr. Taylor's house was next to ours but back a little bit. He lived alone and I only remember going into his house on one occasion, when I was transfixed by a portrait of a lady above the fireplace. Everything about the house was very dark and Victorian.

Moving further along the lane, towards Burnham Beck, stood a big shed owned by Herbert Wilson. The last house on the lane was The White House, where Mr. and Mrs. Jack Johnson lived with their son, David. Mike and I used to play with David until he went away to boarding school. He had sheds full of wartime memorabilia. I remember when he first went away to school, Mike and I put our pocket money together and bought him a bar of McCowan's Highland Toffee from Mrs Naylor's tiny shop in Battlegreen, to put in his tuck box. Mrs. Johnson, David's mother, was a quiet lady who very kindly accepted my offer of a few decades-old lavender bags for a small remuneration. When Granny Ivy and Grandad Bobby Temperton were having Dad's old room converted into a bathroom, an ancient chest was taken out and brought to us at Studcross Cottage. Inside were some very old lavender bags. Being an enterprising child, I took them along the lane to Mrs. Johnson and sold them to her. When Mum found out, she was - quite naturally - rather cross and made me repay the money. I was very embarrassed. That was probably the first time I felt embarrassed. It has happened a lot of times since!

I have wondered why Studcross is so named. I would be happy to be told but meanwhile I have a theory. As a stud was a post, it may have been that, a very long time ago, probably before the drainage, there was a marker to show where the land became marsh - this theory is based on the knowledge that a mere ran between Studcross Lane and Fieldside. The Isle of Axholme was so altered by the drainage that it is impossible to imagine the landscape as it was before the Dutch arrived.

My early years at Studcross Cottage were a source of security and a springboard for life. I belonged there with my parents and younger brother. Sometimes our cousin, Jane, would come to stay for long periods of time when my auntie was ill or when Jane's younger siblings were born. Then I counted myself lucky to have a sort-of-sister.

Starting school at the Easter before I was five changed my young life completely. There was no preparation in nurseries or toddler groups in those days. We were straight out of home and into lessons. If a small person didn't like school then that small person had to lump it. Neither were there special plans drafted up to allow said sad small person to acclimatise to school at his/her own pace. The children, the teachers, the caretaker and the ladies who did secretarial work and playground duty all became a part of who I was in 1958.

Elementary Education

A school was founded in Epworth in 1711 by Henry Clifford, Rector of Wroot, and his wife, Mary, just two years after the terrible fire at Epworth Rectory, when John Wesley was rescued from an upstairs room. Changes were made to the running of the school over many years and, in 1856, education there became free of any charges. The school attended by my grandma (born Florence Mabel Emerson) was in Battlegreen and a little further northwest from the original school. Until 1903 it had been Epworth Board School, the School Board having been formed in 1874 - the year in which the building was erected. Epworth County School was one of two schools existing in Epworth when I started my education. The Church of England Primary School became Saint Andrew's Church Centre and our school became an inn. We also had pupils of secondary age at Epworth County until South Axholme was opened in 1961.

After a summer of thunderstorms in 1957, Easter 1958 was a chilly one but, as a newbie at school, sunshine was everywhere. I remember the Big Storm (anyone a Vicar of Dibley fan?!) in July 1957 - Mr. Gravil's television at Studcross was damaged. If Mum was afraid, she didn't let it show as I am not at all worried about thunder and lightning now - but common sense tells me it is wise to avoid vast open places! We would always make sure there were two windows open in a thunderstorm - to allow the phenomenon to pass through the house without misadventure!

Back to Easter 1958 when I started school with Mrs. Snell as my teacher. Before marrying Colin Snell in 1957, Mrs. Snell was Mirlwyn Atack and her family home was at the end of the lane between Battlegreen and Fieldside - so, in fact, quite close to us at Studcross. It was the term of my fifth birthday and I remember the classroom being fragrant with spring flowers. There were jam jars full of them on every available shelf and ledge. I was nervous, and yet I was drawn into this new world by the kindness of the teacher and of the older children. Mrs. Snell was so patient with each and every one of us. I don't remember her ever raising her voice. But we were, naturally, angelic.

It was a good time to begin our education. The Second World War had gifted us great progress in technology and science. The dynamo powered torch was a good development from wartime technology and was beginning to appear on bicycles up and down the country. In medicine, penicillin was used to solve health problems. Although Alexander Fleming discovered it in 1928, it wasn't until 1939 that Howard Florey demonstrated its potential. The Campaign for Nuclear Disarmament made its Easter march from London to Aldermaston in Berkshire and sang "Brother Won't You Join The Line" at the Atomic Weapons Establishment there.

There had been sad and happy news - and some which would make people think a little bit more about politics. Sadly, seven Manchester United footballers were killed in the Munich air disaster - another died a short while afterwards in hospital. "The Bridge On The River Kwai" won seven awards at the Academy Awards Ceremony and, politically, Nikita Khrushchev became Premier of the Soviet Union. In January 1958, the first artificial satellite, Sputnik 1, ceased its orbit of the earth. People had been able to spot it in the early evenings since its launch by the Russians the previous October. This important development meant that the U.S.A. and Great Britain were to take scientific funding, including for astrophysics, even more seriously from thereon in. Education would benefit from this at all levels. Harold Macmillan was the Tory Prime Minister in Britain - and would remain in office until 1963.

In the world of education, experimental comprehensive schools were opened on urban sites under Labour authorities. The government was fairly hostile to this use of bombsites. It took courage to experiment with education in such a way but the comprehensive system is, at present, still with us.

In my world, school was safe. I'm not a perfect specimen but I was not a naughty child and, when I disappointed, I took my punishment. When I was milk monitor in Miss Trimingham's class I once dropped a bottle and accepted, tearfully, that I had to hand over the badge. My partner in crime - no names! - and I had been running with the trolley, so the dressing-down was deserved. I respected Miss Trimingham. She was firm but fair. But that event was later on. Going back to the infant classroom with Mrs. Snell and then Mrs. Thorpe, we learned to read with "Janet and John", we counted with beads and cowrie shells, we coloured with thick wax crayons and we modelled with plasticine. When we painted, our water was in glass - yes, glass - jars. In fine weather we had physical exercise in the playground, but in the winter, we went weeks with no P.E. or Games at all. At the back of the school was a pleasant garden and occasionally we were allowed to use it. Some teachers would take us outside on glorious summer days but, for me, it was difficult to concentrate out of doors - instead, I would soak up the sounds, sights and smells of my surroundings.

The school house was attached to the school and our headteachers - Mr. Cook with his family and, later, Mr. Wass and his family - lived there. Having recently listened to Drs. Adam Rutherford and Hannah Fry presenting their radio programme, "The Curious Cases of Rutherford and Fry", where they dealt with childhood memories, I am hoping that mine is serving me correctly here but, as I remember, Mr. and Mrs. Cook had a daughter, Mary, and a son, Andrew. I think they moved to Humberstone after leaving Epworth. Mr. and Mrs. Wass had two sons, Jonathan and Jeremy, and the last I heard of Mr. Wass Snr. was that he was living in Scawby. We had a lady in charge of the school for a while, Miss Storey. She terrified us far more than Mr. Cook or Mr. Wass. She was very strict and, because she wasn't going to be with us for very long, she didn't get to know us as individuals.

Sometimes our teachers would take us on nature walks down the Wroot road, through Carrside. In springtime we would look for buds and shoots. We didn't go very far but it was a genuine pleasure to share my corner of Epworth with school friends. The teacher would not have had today's red tape to consider before taking us out - nor would she have had a classroom assistant or a band of willing parents to join in. When the sap was rising and a nature walk beckoned, the planned lessons would wait. It was just so if a child took something of interest into school, a piece of quartz for example. At such times we would learn everything the teacher knew on the subject and her enthusiasm encouraged us to find out more for ourselves.

Mr. Day was the caretaker and stoked the fires which ran the school heating system. In the playground was a huge mound of fuel for that purpose and anyone caught amongst it or being in possession of a piece was duly dealt with. At the other end of the playground was a wall with a high wire fence above it. Balls rarely made their way over the mesh but, on one occasion, a gypsy lady was walking along the path on the other side when one of our number - again no names! - miscalculated his lift and the ball landed heavily in her basket, breaking the plate which sat on top. She gruffly uttered what we believed to be a gypsy curse and our playground high spirits were somewhat modified for a little while afterwards. There were some lovely playtimes too and we were well looked after by Miss Bradwell and Mrs. Bradley. Both ladies would do administrative work at other times. I loved those playtimes when we could exhale and watch our steamy breath disappear into the cold winter morning. Those were the days when the milk tops would stand proud of the bottles and it was a race to see whether the blue tits had helped themselves to the milk before we did. We lined up at a stretch of ice to take turns at sliding - until there were bruises and tears and we were told to stop. I wasn't very good at sliding but I admired those who were.

The nature table in the classroom was capable of holding my attention for quite some time. It was a delight and a valuable source of wonder. Another special feature of my childhood classroom was the bookcase supporting those books from which we were able to choose and to take away for reading at our own pace. Choosing a book was so different from having one allocated. It wasn't an extensive bookcase but, as we had a limited number of books at home in those days, it was a treasure chest. When I was about nine I won a school competition to make and dress a doll. I made Cleopatra. I knitted her hair and used a cheap toy ring to bend into shape to ornament her forehead. I was absolutely thrilled to win a book token. I loved to choose books from the classroom bookshelf but the books I chose with this token would be mine to keep - and I still have them! One of the books is the Ladybird "What To Look For In Autumn". I read it and re-read it. I delighted in the illustrations, many of which I was able to identify with as the nature studies within them were things familiar to me in the Isle of Axholme.

One of the most frequently asked questions by older people was then and still is,

"Do you like school?"

My answer was always, "Yes, thank you."

A while ago I asked that very question of my great-niece. The slight pause, before she answered in the affirmative, reminded me of those days when I had been left on the periphery of my group of friends due to some disagreement or other, making school temporarily less attractive. My niece's little girl had been hurt in the playground by a boy on a bike so her recent experiences of school had not all been positive - resulting in a slight hesitation before replying. Those playtimes when I was left alone were miserable, but the periods of exclusion were brief. We all fell back in soon after we had fallen out. Of course there was some spite, but it was short-lived.

As children, we were told that the crushed centres of rose-hips made "itching powder". It was the thing to do, at the back end of the year, to split open the beautiful berries and take out their stuffing before shoving it down the backs of anyone with a loose collar. Mrs. Carpenter, who taught us in Juniors, took a dim view of this.

A moment of glory for me was when I was praised by Mrs. England, who taught the older children, for being able to spell the word "liquid" and to explain its meaning. I was a bit scared, standing in front of a class of older children - and I guess they would have liked to show me how unimpressed they were - but the praise ensured I continued to learn my weekly spelling lists and helped me with self-belief.

Some of the teachers were part-time or worked as supply teachers. Mrs. Geary came into school once a week and, because of her enthusiasm for seabirds, was given the nickname, "Guillemot". We were such delightful children! Mrs. Geary was married to one of the Epworth butchers. Mrs. Wright and Mrs. Beckett would come in sometimes. Mrs. Tonge taught many of us to knit and to improve our needlework. Margaret Tonge was married to Dad's cousin, Geoff, who followed his father into joinery. As I write this, I look across the room and see his handiwork still - a petite circular coffee table with a shelf underneath for newspapers which was a wedding present to my mum and dad from Geoff and his parents, my Great Auntie Vic (Violet Victoria Hannah née Temperton) and Uncle Wilf who, incidentally, was the brother of my Great Auntie Ethel who married my Grandad Johnson's older brother, Len. With me so far? Don't worry - it is another small world story. Great Auntie Vic was the sister of my father's father and Great-Uncle Len was the brother of my mother's father. Easy-peasy.

Not all of our primary schooling took place in the old school at Battlegreen. After South Axholme Secondary Modern School was opened in 1961, the H.O.R.S.A. site was used for primary education. It was there that I broke the milk bottle! After the Education Act of 1944, the school leaving age was raised to 15 years and so began the "Hutting Operation for the Raising of the School-Leaving Age" (H.O.R.S.A.). Basically, pre-fabricated huts were put up all over Britain to accommodate the extra young people. Epworth's huts were situated between the pair of semis belonging to the Selby family, and Mr. Percy Lindley's bungalow. Another snippet of trivia - many years before this, Percy Lindley had lived in Aston House - where we lived after leaving Studcross Cottage. Percy (1886-1963) was the son of Caroline Dawson and George Lindley. Caroline was the daughter of Hannah Emerson and James Dawson. Hannah's father was Thomas Emerson who was my 4th great-grandfather. I never stop being surprised when I come across such small world stories! I knew that Mum and Dad bought Aston House from Bryan and Kathleen Lindley but I didn't know until very recently that Bryan was Percy's son. The significance is in a well-remembered kindness shown to me as a child at the recommissioned H.O.R.S.A. site when Mr. Percy Lindley, then in a wheelchair, gave me - and some of my young friends - acorns to plant in order to watch them grow into oak trees. He passed them to us through the wire fence. I planted mine at Studcross Cottage but soon afterwards we moved to Aston House. I remember neither wealth nor class but I never forget kindness and, when a person shares hope in living and growing things, that stays with me.

When the new academic year started each September it was quite exciting to have moved up and to know that the term just beginning would end with the celebration of Christmas, although there would be the "tattie-picking" holiday in October of course. The hedgerows - already wearing their faded-summer expression - would provide for the birds and small mammals through the coming months, and the hedgehogs would soon be seeking out piles of leaves in sheltered places. Each autumn Grandad Bobby and I looked for them at Rose Cottage - in the hedge there - but we never disturbed them.

We were climbing the next rung of our learning ladder with each Autumn Term, usually finding our feet in a different classroom with a different teacher - although sometimes we stayed put, depending on numbers. New books and pencils were shared out. We would have a new coat hook in the cloakroom and, very important this one, new responsibilities would be allotted to each of us. We were ready, willing and mostly eager. There was a security in our village schools which settled us for life and prepared us for an increasingly technological world.

Until we moved to Aston House, 92, High Street, Mike and I went home, at the end of each school day, to Studcross Cottage, Battlegreen. Whichever of the Epworth houses we were living in, we spent a great deal of time down Belshaw Lane with our paternal grandparents. When I was thirteen we went back to live there - at a time when there were only fields between our bungalow and my Granny Ivy and Grandad Bobby's cottage. That soon changed so that the impressive dust storms and the lolloping hares, stopping to enjoy the new shoots in the field, became a memory. Our bungalow was just one of many which were infilling and extending all of the Axholme villages.

Bricks and Mortar

I enjoy looking at copies of Helen Allingham's watercolours. I know her cottages are not everyone's cup of tea and may belie the sheer graft needed to run a home and garden in Victorian England, but they are very pretty. There is one particular painting which, local building materials and techniques excepted, provides an insight to the layout of an Isle of Axholme village in former days. It's a scene of a village street in Kent - not as colourful as some of her artwork but an excellent example of the nature of planning in earlier centuries. It reminds me of conversations I had with the older Axholme folk when I was growing up there in the fifties and sixties. Many of them were able to remember the Second Boer War which ended in 1902 - some could remember a time before that and spoke of "the old queen" as if she were their great-aunt. My Grandad Bobby's full name was Reuben George Robert Cecil Temperton. He would have been Reuben after his father (Reuben Temperton 1867-1946) and George was the name of his uncle who was a blacksmith just a few miles from Grantham. It was also the name of the then future King George V who became second in line to the throne after the death of his brother, Albert Victor, in 1892. At that time, in our family, the same names cropped up over and over again, but Robert and Cecil hadn't appeared on that side of the family. As his father was fighting in the Boer War when Grandad was born, "Robert" was probably chosen because of the glowing reputation of Lord Roberts who took over command of the British forces in South Africa, and "Cecil" because of the fame of Cecil Rhodes who had been Prime Minister of Cape Colony and gave his name to Rhodesia - now Zimbabwe. Since Lord Roberts had many Boers - men, women and children - kettled into his concentration camps where a large percentage of them died, and Rhodes was a white supremacist, I'm not a fan of those two namesakes! However, I couldn't be more proud of the man Grandad was. He was kind, loving, thoughtful, patient and a gentleman in the best sense of the word. His understanding of - and respect for - the world of nature had a profound and lasting effect on me. What's in a name anyway?!

When I was small there were many more very old houses standing in the Isle. Even at a young age I felt sad when old houses were pulled down. Near the site of the 1711 school stood an old building which may have been a house or it may have been a barn - it was difficult to tell because it was well garlanded with ivy. When we walked by, I would watch the birds flying in and out - it had not been a home for people for a very long time, but it provided shelter for birds and small mammals until it disappeared in favour of more modern homes. "Condemned!" was the response when I protested about the fate of these buildings. I remember noticing the braces or anchor plates on the outside walls of older properties - houses and barns - when the weight of the building had caused the walls to bow. They were fixed to a tie-rod or a large bolt and denoted a building of some age. They are still visible on a few properties in the Isle. The old folk would reminisce about the cottages and farms of their childhood. I just loved to listen and, when they looked into the far distance and said, "You don't want to hear me blathering on about them days," I would be disappointed. That was exactly what I did want to hear! As I grew a little bit older, I realised that, with patience, I was quite likely to find out more at a later date! I couldn't get enough local history. Some of it has stayed with me but I wish I had written it all down.

I loved our early homes for their own sakes - and I include Granny's and Grandad's home down Belshaw Lane here. I now realise that a little of myself was left behind in each one.

Gardens and gardening have always featured in my family. Grandad Bobby worked as a gardener for Doctor Macgregor until the good doctor died on Grandad's birthday in 1964. Grandad continued working for Mrs. Macgregor and also for her mother, Mrs. Sharpe, when they lived next door to each other on Burnham Road in Epworth. (Dr. and Mrs. Macgregor had previously lived close by the traffic lights.) Grandad also worked in Doctor Mitchell's garden in Belton as well as keeping his own little Eden at Rose Cottage. Grandad Johnson kept an immaculate garden, first - in my lifetime that is - at the gatehouse on Jeffrey Lane in Belton, gardening along the bank of the railway as well as in his own plot and, later, in Keadby. It was one of those "not a weed in sight" type of gardens. A garden planned with military precision. My later exploration into the grown-up world of kitten heels rendered Grandad's lawn out of bounds for me! We benefitted generously from both grandfathers' produce - fruit, vegetables, salads and cut flowers.

When Mike and I were both at school, Mum set to work on the garden at Studcross where before we'd had just a few plants to keep it cheerful - pansies are the ones I remember most for their irrepressible high spirits. I still think they are smiling at me! After moving to Aston House she had a well laid out garden to work on - the Lindleys had also enjoyed their green space - but Mum had some crazy-paving put down at the bottom of the garden there - behind a little beech hedge. There was a rose-covered archway connecting two short stretches of beech and, in the summer, those red roses combined wonderfully with cream astilbe - also taken from the garden - to make an indoor display. Mum has always been able to create lovely arrangements with flowers.

I don't remember using the front door at Studcross very often, we mostly used the back door. The path was made of old bricks until the concrete was put down - that was such an exciting day - perhaps we used the front door on that day. I remember planks of wood being set up as a bridge over the wet cement so that we could get to the toilet. Ours was in the back yard. It was a wooden bench, with a hole in it, set above a large metal drum which caught everything - including the newspaper - we didn't use toilet paper until we moved to Aston House. There was always a pile of newspaper next to the seat but it was so dark in there that it clearly wasn't for reading. And *you* thought the black bottom was a dance from the 1920s! Once a week the dilly-cart men would come and empty the soil-pan and, on those days, Mike and I were whisked inside with our toys until the men had gone and Mum had swilled the path with a disinfectant solution. The good old days. Granny Ivy and Grandad Bobby had a slightly more sophisticated loo in that their soil-pan had a seat attached to the outer drum - still needed emptying each week though. Eventually they converted Dad's old room into a bathroom and had a flush toilet - magic! When we moved to Aston House we were in a different world where sanitation was concerned. Not only did we have TWO flushing toilets (although one was outside) but we also had a bath. The bathroom itself was very roomy and had old-fashioned rubber tiles on the floor which should have deadened the noise, but I remember the wonderful sound quality when anyone sang in the bath - it made a little diva out of a dabbler. Our Studcross baths had been portable ones taken in front of the kitchen fire with our nightclothes warming on the fireguard. We knew nothing else. It all seemed quite normal.

 Going up the stairs to bed was spooky at Studcross. There was a door in the kitchen which opened straight onto the steps and, unless a bedroom door had been left open, there was no natural light in there. At the top of the stairs and on the right were two doors - one to my brother's room and one to my parents' room. On the left was the door to my room. My bedroom, although it was accessed from the house, was not really above it but above the old barn where my mum did the washing every Monday. I had two windows in my little room. One looked over our property towards Battlegreen and the other over fields to The White House and onwards in the direction of Burnham Beck. We didn't go upstairs during the day unless we were very poorly. I remember being ill and listening to men harvesting with the reaper-binder in the field at the other side of the mere. By that time the machinery was pulled by a tractor but some of the carts which rattled up and down our lane had originally been pulled by horses. The carts were very old but well cared for. Mr. Mell, pipe in mouth, would drive up the lane rather steadily on his tractor with the wonderful wooden cart following in a most precarious manner. You could imagine he was coaxing the tractor over the bumps as if it were a horse or a pair. One man and his tractor! The Mells lived at Carrside and had farmed there even before the railway had dissected their land.

Sheaves of corn were stood on end in stooks after harvesting and, during the time they waited to be collected, we would play amongst them. The corn was sweet smelling and warm and the stubble was prickly. Pigeons, who are still opportunists in my Far North garden, were there for the gleanings.

Sometimes the Chapel Sunday School outings went past on a cart, or on the back of a lorry, with the children singing their happy hymns. That was so exciting - we didn't get much traffic down our lane. Our little house was a bit out of the way, but not isolated. When Mike and I hung out of his bedroom window on warm, light summer nights, there would be a well-meaning neighbour knocking on the door to tell Mum. We'd been spotted and we were in trouble! In the coldest winters I was moved from my draughty little bedroom into Mike's room. This had the chimney breast going through it and so was a bit warmer. Without central-heating we were able to look, when we got up in the mornings, for the patterns which Jack-Frost had painted onto the window panes. I remember the swirls and the ferns and how they merged into a marvellous ice tapestry. The house seemed to be a living thing and not just a place for living in.

When Mum was occupied with something else, Mike and I would sometimes lift the lino in the kitchen and watch the worms wriggling between the bricks underneath. The lino by the back door was the best place for this. It peeled back there relatively simply without cracking. It is surprising how easily an oil-based material will crack - and how quickly a grown-up can spot it! Other living creatures included mice. Every effort was made to get rid of the little blighters but they were, in fact, a blight and a menace and a pest and I can think of many more words to describe them from a housewife's viewpoint, but they shared our home from time to time as they had shared the homes of our forebears for centuries. We knew when they were around because we found their tiny footprints in the fat which was left to set in the frying pan on the gantry shelf. The shelf was built of brick and painted in a deep red masonry paint. It ran along one wall of the pantry which was underneath my bedroom. The pantry itself was accessed through the "best room" (only in use on special occasions) and was very cold, with half of the window covered in a fine metal mesh.

So, one could go in through the back door, cross the kitchen - which, as well as being our bathroom, was also our living room and dining room - and out through the front door. Not ideal but we rarely used the front door so the potential gale was not a problem. On the gable end wall of the kitchen was a pot sink and next to it was the fireplace. The door to upstairs was in the corner there. We didn't have fitted carpets - in fact we didn't have carpets - we had rugs which Mum had made, sometimes with the help of Mrs. Otley who would come and work with her, after we had gone to bed, in the long winter evenings.

Dad started to build up a farm produce business in the early sixties, firstly with Walter Law in Epworth, at a site behind Mr. Law's house on Church Street, and then - on his own - in Belton. Washed carrots paved the way for washed potatoes. In summer he bought crops of peas and beans and employed gangs to pull them - this was before pea viners - sending the bags to the big markets. It went well and so we left Studcross Cottage for a larger house on Epworth High Street. Aston House was quite different. It was easy to identify the three periods of its construction. The part with the old bricks was in between the front of the house and the newer stretch of outhouses leading to the garden. The first outhouse was attached to the kitchen and contained a boiler from former wash days. Going down towards the garden was an outdoor loo which flushed - but not in the big freeze of 1963 when the water became ice and stayed that way for some time. Attached was the coal house and next to that was a pig sty which was so clean that it had probably never been used for a pig - we certainly never kept one. My friend, Anne, and I played house there and that is where I tried to nurse poorly birds - and failed miserably!

Exactly opposite from us was an elegant pair of houses. They were an older type of semi-detached property. Facing them from Aston House, the house on the left was lived in by John Selby and his parents and on the right lived Stephen Selby with his parents. Their joint plot went all the way back to Fieldside and some very interesting agricultural machinery was kept there.

Our new home was entirely different from our cottage. The bathroom was not the only novelty. We had carpets and fresh new wallpaper with curtains to match. There were two sitting rooms, one on either side of a hallway bedecked in Lincrusta and with a high shelf running all around it. Mum enjoyed collecting plates and decorative jugs to sit on the shelf, and Uncle Wilf - who sold antiques as a hobby - found some delightful items for her. The large living kitchen at the back was always warm as we had an Esse stove. Mum cooked wonderful meals in there. We had, for the first time, an electric washing machine and a fridge. And no more chamber pots under the beds! But perhaps the strangest passion for a child still at primary school was my fascination with the pantry. We had a pantry at Studcross with the required gantry and a meat safe and a window with metal mesh - but the pantry at Aston House was something else. It wasn't a thin strip of a room along the back of the barn as the one at Studcross had been. It was square and room-sized with perfect tiles on the floor and shiny ones on the walls. The walls were shelved in melamine and there was a globe light in there, close to the ceiling, so that it was never dark. The window gave light in the daytime. I watched Mum fill up the shelves when we moved in - pots and glasses also went in there - with room to spare. I delighted in the neat rows of various jams which appeared in summer and early autumn. Each week, after shopping, I watched her replace the used food items and I felt a sense of security and pleasure. Those feelings have stayed with me. I am still satisfied when I put away the food shopping or make a batch of jam or chutney and my fridge, freezer and food cupboards are full. Guilt creeps in over the excess at Christmas but, at other times of the year, it is just nice to know that we are well-stocked.

Granny Ivy's pantry was slightly lower than her tiny scullery. Entering there felt as if you were descending into the bowels of the earth. It was dark and perhaps the coldest room I have ever been in. Pantries or larders were a must in the days before ordinary folk like us acquired a fridge. And they worked.

Food kept well in those places and flies were never found there because the temperature stayed low all year round due to their position and structure. Most people I knew kept a mouse trap. We buy the humane ones now - which you take away and empty, rushing to make sure you get back home before the mouse does!

Rose Cottage was special because it had been in the Temperton family for many years. It was a terrible wrench for Granny and Grandad when they left, but there seemed to be no sense in them struggling to upkeep the house and garden when they had the opportunity to go to a comfortable and convenient bungalow in Churchtown. The stairs at Rose Cottage were very steep and not easy to negotiate - especially with arms full of laundry, or a vacuum cleaner. Goodness knows how ladies in olden days, with their voluminous dresses, carried their babies and sick children up and down. The bedrooms had very low ceilings. People didn't spend time in their bedrooms unless they were in bed. One of the bedrooms had a large open cupboard over the stairs. Granny had a curtain drawn across it and, when I stayed overnight, I tried to forget that it was there. It was dark and creepy. The opposite bedroom was Granny's and Grandad's and eventually they had a bathroom - after they had converted Dad's old room which opened off theirs.

Downstairs there was a best room on the right as you reached the bottom. It was always kept nicely and not used very often, but I remember some very happy times in there at Christmas. On the left was the living room, which was used for baking, eating, resting at the end of the day in front of a blazing fire, listening to the radio and, later, watching the television. If you were a naughty boy - as my dad apparently was on occasions – you were sent into the cupboard under the stairs until you were able to behave yourself. Through the living room was the scullery and through that was the pantry. The house didn't stop there. Joined to it was a barn at the scullery side and at the opposite side, next to the best room, was a toilet and a shed built behind it. This was close to where the hens were kept and, behind them was an ancient and dilapidated cart shed which was used to house Grandad's car. I loved the smell of the old brick barn. It spoke to me of generations of my own family, all of whom had loved this place. Lassie, the collie, had an old sack in the barn where she slept. She also had a place in the lawn where she had made a form for her frequent naps. The food for the chickens was kept in the barn as well as all manner of implements which I was advised to leave on their stout hooks and nails. I was terrified of Grandad's great scythe. He made it look light and easy to operate - I'm sure it wasn't.

Our branch of the Temperton family moved from West Butterwick and Owston Ferry to Belton around 1785 with William, my 4th great-grandfather, and his wife, Ann Brewitt. William was born at West Butterwick and baptised at Saint Martin's, Owston Ferry, in 1759. One of their sons was Reuben, my 3rd great-grandfather, who was baptised at All Saints' Church, Belton on 26th September, 1791. He married Elizabeth Mitchell from Crowle and they lived in Hag Lane by Woodhouse, Belton. By 1861 our family had moved over to the other side of the village with my great-great-grandfather, John (baptised 25th September 1830), who lived first at Churchtown and then was living at Carrhouse (Belshaw Lane) in 1871 until the time of his death in 1895. John was married to Hannah Watkinson from Owston Ferry. All of their descendants gravitated to Rose Cottage for regular visits until it was sold in the early 1980s.

The garden was paradise. There was an orchard, fruit bushes too, and a large cherry tree by the scullery window. There were grassy paths separating the different parts of the garden, an old water pump next to a big privet - just one privet but a grand specimen - and a vegetable plot running between the lane and Grandad's cart shed. Loganberries grew along the back of the house and, wherever you walked, you felt an awareness that here was the best care that humankind could give to the Garden of Eden.

These are three childhood homes I have loved - two of our homes in Epworth and Granny's and Grandad's home in Belton. The bricks and mortar were secondary to the peace and security they offered.

Memory is a funny thing. Every so often I will remember something which, until that point, appeared to have been lost. How does that happen? Of my parents' ancestors, only two branches had lived in the Isle for centuries - the Tempertons - my Dad's father's side, and the Emersons - my Mum's mother's side. It is remarkable how many local families are tied in with these two branches. I hope I can put together a little history so that those with links to the Isle of Axholme will realise our families were once neighbours or that we may even be related! People who have more recently settled in the Isle will recognise the names of families they have come to know.

Over the Garden Gate

Ingredients: 1 teacupful linseed, 2d.Spanish liquorice, 6ozs raisins, 2 quarts water.
Boil slowly until reduced to about half, add twopennyworth of brown sugar candy, when dissolved, strain,add a little lemon juice.

An odd way to start! I copied this recipe, exactly as printed, for "John Wesley's Cough Mixture", from "The 1928 Cookery Book" issued by the Barton Wesleyan Bazaar Committee. This little book belonged to my husband's grandmother. The reason I have included it here is because I hope that "Over The Garden Gate" places us all together in one big pot. Anyone who is from the Isle of Axholme, or has had any connection at all with it, knows about John Wesley and his rather amazing family. I'll bet every single one of us can recognise at least one hymn by Charles - although we may not realise he wrote it - and we've probably seen Samuel Snr.'s tomb in Epworth churchyard. Years ago I read everything I could get my hands on about Susanna Wesley and her daughters. With all the information out there about the Wesley family, it is easy to forget that they actually *lived* amongst our ancestors in Axholme. Those born in the Isle - and those who have come to call Axholme "home" - all have John Wesley in common. The reference to linseed is relevant too as many of us have historical connections with the growing and dressing of flax. Our ancestors are unlikely to have known about Omega 3 fatty acids, but flax put bread and butter on their tables, fuel on their fires and clothes on their backs.

Keith can trace his family, on his mother's side, back to the Norman conquest - but not me. Goodness knows when our mixed bunch became worthy of records. Although some branches of my family are not from North Lincolnshire, the Emersons and Tempertons have lived in the Isle of Axholme for generations.

My sixth great-grandfather Emerson was Robert, and we think he came from elsewhere in Lincolnshire. The furthest back we have been able to get a definite record for one of our Emersons born in the Isle is 1748 when my fifth great-grandfather, William, was born in Epworth. William's mother was probably of Dutch descent. She was called Hannah and came from Haxey. Her surname may have been Hybord or Hubbard. Interestingly, William married Mary Gleading, who was also likely to have had Dutch ancestors - which may account for the height of the Emersons, generally a tall family. Perhaps these families with Dutch ancestry are descended from Vermuyden's workforce. It wasn't only Frank Vavasour and Anna Goel who had relationships which crossed lines - thankfully - or we would be inbred by now with associated genetic problems!

Probably / may have been / likely / perhaps - my hypothesis of the Dutch ancestors is based only on fragments of knowledge and I am aware that these can be misleading. However, much of what follows is verifiable through the documentary evidence which remains.

The census of 1851 is an interesting one in relation to the Emersons of Battle Green, Epworth. In that year my great-great-grandfather, Thomas Emerson (1838-1892) was a young lad of twelve and lived in Battle Green (here Battle Green is two words) with his parents, George (1816-1900) and Hannah (1819-1856). Thomas and his ten year old brother, William, worked alongside their father as dealers in flax. Their seven year old brother, Young, and five year old brother, George, are described as scholars. They also had a two year old sister, Mary Hannah, and a baby brother, Eli. In this 1851 census, when George and

Hannah Emerson lived in Battle Green with their young family, George's father, also Thomas (1789-1853), and George's mother, Mary (1796-1872), lived in Battle Green too. Thomas Snr. is recorded as a farmer in both the 1841 and 1851 censuses.

Another Mary (née Shipley) Emerson, a twenty-nine year old straw bonnet maker, lived with her son, Robert, in Battle Green at that time. She was the widow of James Emerson. I have collected some familiar names from the 1851 census - the year of the Great Exhibition at Crystal Palace in London and also the year when the miserable window tax was abolished. (You can still see evidence - where windows were blocked in - of the window tax on some of the older properties around the Isle.) My list of the Emersons' neighbours in the Battle Green of 1851 needs to be limited but I have chosen a few which should ring bells - Epworth Bells! "Ring out the old, ring in the new . . . . . Ring out the false, ring in the true". They are Balmforths, Chafers, Clarks, Coggans, Fosters, Glews, Gravels, Johnsons, Shaws, Taylors and - yes - Tempertons.

Thomas senior (born 1789) and Mary Emerson were, at that time, living with their sons, John and Charles, their daughter, Sarah, and married daughter, Eliza Brown. Living with them were Eliza's husband, Thomas Brown, and their baby son, Emerson Brown, aged 3 months.

The Gravel family (also flax dealers) in Battle Green, named their son Emerson Gravel. This is getting a little bit confusing - we have the Emerson family and also the Brown family - with an Emerson aged 3 months. We also have the Gravel family with a Young Emerson. Christopher Gravel's wife, Harriet (1818-1892), was another daughter of Thomas and Mary Emerson. Emerson Gravel later married Emily Ward. They had one daughter, Harriet, who died aged thirteen, and is buried in Epworth with her grandparents Susannah and William Ward. Emerson Gravel's older brother, John and his wife Emily, named their son

Emerson too. This younger Emerson Gravel in turn named *his* son Herbert Emerson Gravel. The Emersons were not going to be forgotten!

By 1891 - the year when London and Paris were first connected by telephone - George (1816-1900) was living in Low Burnham with his third wife, Jane, from West Ferry, and was a cordwainer (shoemaker). Earlier, in the 1841 census, before he became a flax dealer, he was described as a cordwainer. In the first half of the nineteenth century, plans were made for factories to be built in Lincolnshire for the purpose of processing flax. It may be George had high hopes of flax dealing, then, being disappointed when it became apparent that the factory plans were very limited, went back to his former craft. In Low Burnham, George and Jane Emerson lived next door to Samuel and Sarah Chapman who ran the pub at that time. (Earlier in the century it was Tempertons who were the publicans in Burnham.) On their other side was the Carter family. Mr. Carter was a farm produce merchant.

After the death of his first wife, Hannah, early in 1856, George Emerson was not a widower for very long and later that year he married Ann, the widow of the local schoolmaster, Mr. Barrow. George's third wife, Jane, was the daughter of John Scholey, a sawyer, and his wife, Jane (formerly Holgate), who became a schoolmistress to support her young family on the death of her husband in 1850. When George Emerson married the younger Jane, she was working as a field labourer to support herself and her daughter, Alice. The Burnham connection goes on as, after George's death in 1900, his grandson, Robert (1879-1954), my great-grandfather, was living in Burnham for the birth of his fourth son, William Henry, in 1906. He lived at the railway gatehouse there, with his wife, Blanche (née Taylor 1876-1955), and their five sons at the time of the 1911 census. They were to have another two sons and a daughter - my grandma. There were no near neighbours at the gatehouse. It was really outside Burnham and along the railway track from Epworth.

Another link with Burnham for us was my great-aunt, Gert. Auntie Gert lived there when I was growing up. She was born Gertrude Brown and was the daughter of Jabez Brown, born in Epworth, and his wife, Hannah. Auntie Gert (1897-1989) was married to Grandad Bobby's brother, Alfred Claude Shores Temperton (1898-1951). They farmed at Carrhouse, Belton, and then at Wroot Grange until Alfred's death. I remember the very old farmhouse at Wroot when Alfred and Gert's son, my godfather, Peter Temperton, and his wife, Maud, lived there after Alfred's death. Auntie Maud was my godmother, as was my Auntie Gwen (Dad's sister).

I don't think there is a single village in the Isle of Axholme with which I have no family association. Test me and I will search out an ancestor or someone closely connected with an ancestor.

I started my family tree research when I was about thirteen - more than half a century ago. I found it quite difficult at first to find out anything from my grandparents. My Grandma Johnson (born Florence Mabel Emerson) was able to tell me every little detail about those alive at the time - with names of families linked to ours thrown in for good measure - names such as Havercroft and Aldam - but no details of *how* we are linked. It really didn't matter to Grandma. Family was family - regardless of how the attachment was formed. She did whatever she could to help those who were in any way related to her and may have been in need. However, this inability to make the connections for me was a bit like being given a corked bottle of water in the desert - with no corkscrew. It can be argued that Grandma's generosity - for example, giving a bed to those without one - was of far more value than my research - of course it was.

Granny Ivy Temperton spoke of her father, Jack, although his given name was James Hudson, from Bainton in Yorkshire - and her mother, Janet, born Janetta Mary Richardson in Middlesborough. Granny could remember her Aunt Rebecca - her mother's sister. Thanks to social media I am now a friend of Rebecca's granddaughter. We grew up many miles apart but we have much in common. Although there is a difference of one generation, we are close in age. We are of the same Cayley/Richardson stock. Granny Ivy's family came from East Yorkshire and, before that, from Suffolk and further afield. Granny's three older sisters and her older brother were all born in Yorkshire but she was born in Luddington. The family later moved to Belton. I love to remember Granny's giggle - her whole face lit up - and she did this when I tried to probe into her family history - she was so amused by my interest.

Grandad Johnson's family were from West Yorkshire, moving to the Isle of Axholme at the beginning of the twentieth century and living in Epworth, where Grandad was born, for a short time until his father, Charles Fenwick Johnson, became Station Master at Luddington with Garthorpe, moving then to Haldenby. My great-grandparents later took their family south to Haxey. They stayed there, Charles and Emma, until their deaths. Great-Grandad Charles died in 1956 and Great-Grandma Emma died in 1962.

For a time, Granny Ivy Temperton looked after the Baptist Chapel on Station Road, Epworth - at this time living in a cottage between the chapel and the schoolroom. Great-Uncle Wilf (Wilfred Tonge, 1905-1986) and Auntie Vic (Violet Victoria Hannah née Temperton, 1905-1988) were stalwarts of the Baptist Church in Epworth and lived not far away - just by the railway bridge - over the road from the station. Joined to them were Gervas Tonge (1880-1967) and his wife, Ida, who died in 1968. (Ida was the sister of Billy Taylor, our near neighbour at

Studcross.) On the same side as Auntie Vic and Uncle Wilf, going up the road in the direction of Sandtoft, was where my great-grandparents, Robert and Blanche Emerson, went to live after they left Burnham Gatehouse. They died within a year of each other when I was very small.

The small cottage attached to their house was where their youngest son, Great-Uncle Walt and Auntie Minnie (from Portrush, Country Antrim) lived when they were first married. They later moved to Fox Covert Lane in Misterton.

When I was a child in the 50s and 60s, Browns, the farmers, lived on the next two farmhouses. David and Trevor, who were cousins, were at Epworth County Primary School at the same time as me. I remember one Baptist Sunday School party when we were allowed to play in the field belonging to the Browns. It was across the road from the chapel and we had great fun avoiding the cow pats. I don't think we all managed to get away scot-free. Health and Safety would have a *field* day with that now! Later on, I went to the Church of England Sunday School on Pashley Walk. There was no place for sectarianism in our family. It was more about geography than anything else - Studcross was nearer to the Baptist Chapel, and Aston House was closer to Pashley Walk and Saint Andrew's Church.

Also on Station Road and fairly close to the Chapel - but on the opposite side - was Mr. and Mrs. Bell's grocery shop where we were able to buy homemade iced lollies which Mrs. Bell made from Vimto. I'm still pleased to find Vimto on offer in our local supermarket! It was available in 1908 when my grandparents were small. Originally a herbal tonic which offered "vim" and "vigour", it was named "Vimtonic" and later abbreviated.

Turning round and heading back towards Epworth, the Station House was on the left - up from the railway bridge. The Johnson family (no relation to my Johnson branch) lived there. The children were Peter and Wendy. Wendy and I used to play together until her family moved to Wetherby. There is a photo in existence of us playing in the old baby bath in our garden. Most children have a paddling pool now but in those days we were lucky to have an old bath to play in. This one was circular and was enamelled - like a gigantic mixing bowl. On the Epworth side of the railway bridge, just beyond the station, lived the Stafford family - the children were David and Jill. David and I were in the same year group at school. Next to them lived Great-Uncle Len (1905-1977) and Auntie Ethel (1910-1999), with my mum's cousin, Rodney (1942-1994). Rodney was a great Scunthorpe United football fan - never missed a game.

This has taken us back to Battlegreen - where the Emersons lived years before. The Emersons were mostly associated with the area in and around Battlegreen, but my great-great-grandfather, Thomas, lived, at one time (1881 census) in Hollingsworth Lane, Epworth. He was married to Elizabeth (Eliza) Atkin from Goulceby, near Louth. In 1881 their neighbours included local families such as the Bramhills, Garners, Hills, Hudsons, Matthews and Rimmingtons as well as the Police Superintendent and his wife - and a prisoner from Scotland! The Emersons have also, at various points in time, lived on the High Street in Epworth too.

The first Temperton we can be sure was born in the Isle of Axholme is William, who was baptised in Owston Ferry in 1698, his family living, at that time, in West Butterwick. We believe his father was John but are, at the time of writing, unsure of where John was born. We also think William had a brother named Joseph who was baptised in 1694. William married Jane and it was their son, also William, who is my fifth great-grandfather. This William, a blacksmith, married Eleanor in 1755 in Messingham and they had two children - William and Mary - before Eleanor died and William married again, having further children. Messingham is not far from West Butterwick. The river crossing was not a problem then but none of us would think of it now. The younger William was born in West Butterwick and baptised in Owston Ferry in 1759. He married Ann Brewitt in 1783 and their children were born and grew up in Belton. He was living at Carr House in Belton at the time of the 1841 census. He either lived with or next door to his daughter, Eleanor Machin, and her youngest son, Thomas. Eleanor was a field labourer as was her ten year old son. William's other neighbours in Carr House (two words on the census) in 1841, the year before his death, included Arrands, Leggotts, Markhams, Surrs and Winters.

In that year the British were fighting in Afghanistan and wagon trains were making their way across America to settle in California. The new Queen Victoria gave birth to her second child, Albert Edward, later King Edward VII, in November of that year. Her first child, Victoria Adelaide Mary Louisa, had been born the year before. I have to admit to more than just a little mind-wandering when I am researching family history - I try to imagine what life was like for my ancestors and how current affairs may have affected them - or not. I can say, hand on heart, that searching for details of those who came before me has had only positive effects. Yes, I have shed tears for their tragedies but, even so, I feel that my sorrow is like a little prayer for the souls of those to whom I owe much. Practically it is a great hobby too - motoring around Britain and pulling on a pair of wellies to investigate an overgrown graveyard, for instance, is, perhaps surprisingly, uplifting - especially when things are in bloom and the birds are vocal. As I write this, the lilac is opening up in our garden and I remember Sunday-visiting with my Grandma Johnson in her little Morris Minor and, later, in her Volkswagen Beetle. We would return with arms full of double white and lilac in fifty shades for May!

The census I am going to focus on for the Tempertons is the 1911 census. 1911 was the year of the coronation of King George V and Queen Mary, and also the year when RMS Titanic was launched in Belfast. Grandad Bobby was able to remember the sinking of the Titanic in April 1912 on her maiden voyage from Southampton to New York City. He had clearly been moved by the tragedy when he was a twelve year old, as he spoke of it with such sadness and compassion. Another interesting fact for 1911 was the birth of Chad Varah in Barton on Humber, North Lincolnshire. Chad Varah founded the Samaritans after officiating at the funeral of a young girl who had taken her own life. Towards the end of his life he was not always happy with the changing direction of the organisation. North Lincolnshire has produced some truly great sons and daughters, but they don't all have their names in the history books.

My great-grandfather (Reuben Temperton, 1867-1946) and my great-grandmother (Louisa - born Dimbleby in Faldingworth, Lincolnshire, 1869-1924) farmed at "Carr House, Belton, near Doncaster" in 1911. They lived there with their three surviving sons (they had lost twin boys in 1903 and 1904) and with two of their three daughters. By this time Elizabeth Blanche Temperton (later to marry John W. Hirst) was working for the Bowman family, in Beltoft, as a live-in domestic servant. Also living with Reuben and Louisa was 19 year old Fred Paulger who was working as a farm servant. Fred was the son of Eliza, the older sister of Louisa.

There were some familiar names down Carrhouse in 1911 too - Clark, Fox, Haslehurst, Holmes, Jackson, Johnson, Leggott and Surr. I have picked out just a few. Mostly people there worked the fertile land. Arthur Temperton and his wife Mary also lived in Carrhouse in 1911. Arthur, who died in 1951, was the brother of Reuben and, when I was a child, he was referred to with great affection. In 1911 - in the fields between Belshaw Lane and the old railway - and little more than a stone's throw from where Mum and Dad later built their bungalow - Fred and Louisa Widdowson lived at Primrose Hill with their three month old baby - also Fred. Louisa (born in 1887 in Malton, North Yorkshire) was known in the family as Lily and was the daughter of Eliza, Louisa Temperton's sister, making her half-sister to Fred Paulger. When we lived at Branscombe Lodge, Belshaw Lane, Belton, I would sometimes walk along the path of the old railway and, on occasions, I would make a detour, popping into the ruinous building at Primrose Hill. It had a story to tell but I had no idea at the time that someone from my family had lived there. A barn owl roosted in the old house and sometimes bags of what may have been fertiliser or lime were stored inside the walls. Fred Widdowson Snr., fighting with the Lincolnshire Regiment, died of his wounds in France in October 1915. Louisa, or Lily, was married again in 1918 to John Nicholson of Epworth who was a neighbour of Eliza Emerson, the widow of Thomas Emerson and mother of my great-grandfather, Robert Emerson. John Nicholson also fought with the Lincolnshire Regiment in France during the First World War. So many associations. Each time I identify a link I realise afresh how we are all really one big family.

In the previous census (1901) Reuben was not at home. He was fighting in the second Boer War and it was Louisa who topped the list of household members. In 1885 Reuben had enlisted in the Lincolnshire Regiment at the age of eighteen and is described as a soldier on his marriage certificate (1891). He distinguished himself and, when the Great War began in 1914, he was a recruiting sergeant.

Three of Reuben's siblings were still living at the time of the 1911 census - one was Arthur, mentioned above - the others were John and Edwin. John was living with his second wife,

Mary (née Bassindale, from Belton), in Althorpe and working as a farm labourer. Edwin was living in Finchley, London, and was a bookseller for the Quakers. He had previously been a Salvation Army preacher in Warwickshire and Buckinghamshire. Edwin was a communicator and a man of principle.

An interesting little bit of trivia from an earlier census - 1871 - is that John Temperton (1829-1895), father of Reuben, was a near neighbour of Watson Markham in Carr House, Belton. At that time John was living with his wife, Hannah (1832-1883), their sons, John, Edwin and Reuben, and daughters, Sophia and Hannah Elizabeth. Watson Markham, a boot and shoe maker, was my great-great-great-grandfather - the grandfather of Blanche Taylor (daughter of Mary Ann Markham and Thomas Taylor from Timberland near Tattershall) who married Robert Emerson. Yet another small-world story.

The difficulty with this family tree thing is that I never know when to stop! I wonder, for example, who a direct ancestor's sister married and start to research - and keep on researching until I find out. You might think that is straight forward enough, but the search takes me all over maps and across time. If I see a name I recognise, for any reason at all, I am capable of going way off course - but I have learned such a lot on the journey. However, it becomes more and more difficult to process this new knowledge and I am constantly referring to my notes but, once they are collated, they remain for posterity.

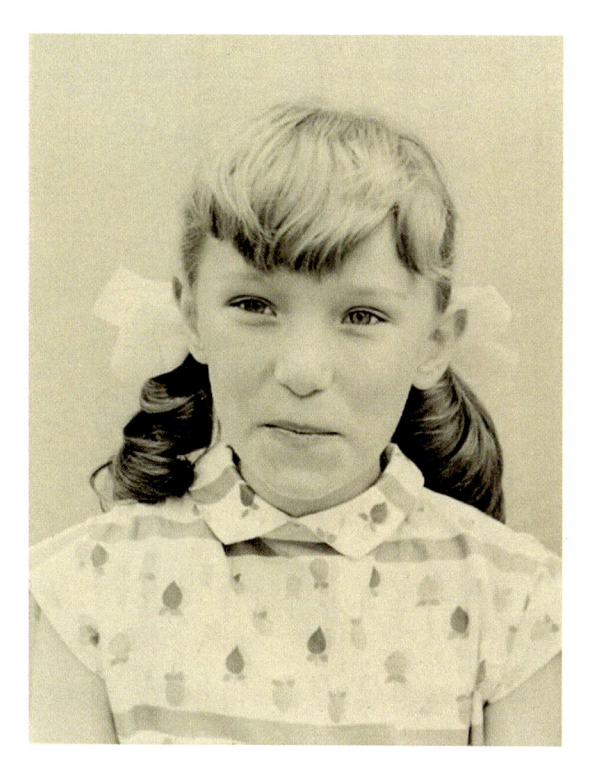

My School Photograph, Early Juniors

			BAPTISM CERTIFICATE.				Page	
	Baptism solemnized in the Parish of Belton			in the Diocese of Lincoln		and County of Lincoln		in the Year 1953
Alleged date of Birth	When Baptised	Child's Christian Name	Parents' Names		Abode	Quality, Trade, or Profession	God-Parents' Names	By whom the Sacrament was administered
			Christian	Surname				
19th June 1953	30th August 1953	Susan Linda	George Reuben & June Margaret	Temperton	Carr House Belton	Potato Salesman		G Hansford

I Certify, that the foregoing is a true Copy of the entry of the Baptism of Susan Linda Temperton in the Register of Baptisms for the said Parish of Belton

Dated this 30 day of August 19 53   Signed G Hansford

With my godmother and Dad's sister, Auntie Gwen, on her wedding day, 1955

Grandma and Grandad Johnson on their wedding day, 1931

Mum and Dad on their wedding day, 1952 (see page 117)

PRESENTATION TO SGT R. TEMPERTON

A LARGE and enthusiastic audience gathered together in Belton Public Hall on Monday evening last to welcome and also witness the presentation to Sergeant Temperton of a marble timepiece, the cost of which had been raised by subscriptions.

The proceedings opened with a pianoforte solo by Mrs Standring, after which S. H. C. Ashlin, Esq., J.P., who presided, said he was glad to see so many present. They were pleased to see him looking so well after the dangers, hardships and privations he had undergone. Mr C. Godfrey said Sgt Temperton was one of those who had borne the brunt of war and fought well for the King and Government.

My great-grandfather, Reuben Temperton and a cutting from *The Epworth Bells* "Milestones of the Past"

Grandad Bobby (seated) and his older brother, Great Uncle Alfred Temperton

Grandma and
Grandad Johnson

Grandma and
Grandad
Temperton

My class at Epworth County School
(I'm 2nd from left, front row)

Florence Mabel Emerson (Grandma Johnson),
4th from left, front row, Epworth County School

Belton Parish Church magazine, Epworth August 1955, the issue which includes the baptism of Michael Andrew

Mike's ink drawing of Wesley Memorial Methodist Church

Rose Cottage, Belton, notice the anchor plates either side of the window on the right

1900 The baby is my Grandad Bobby with mother, Louisa, sister, Blanche and brothers, Joseph and Alfred

Great-Grandma and Great-Grandad Emerson on holiday in Blackpool

Cousin Jane, in the pram, with yours truly at Studcross Cottage

Mike, Jane and me at Studcross Cottage, early sixties

Grandad William Johnson (left) with brother, Leonard 1907/08

Summertime and Sunny Smiles

At the Baptist Sunday School we were given a booklet of snapshots depicting smiling children from different countries of the world. We showed them to our families and neighbours and they were invited to choose one of the pictures in exchange for a small sum of money. The person donating was invited to jot down their name and address on a stub and their money was put to good use, perhaps for missionary work or for the National Children's Homes. These photographs were aptly named "Sunny Smiles". The smiles which were sold first were often babies and the older children had to wait to be chosen. A bit of a shame but I'm sure the money raised benefited every one of those children. I'm not at all sure that we were given these in the summer but the memory of them makes me think of sunshine.

I love the Ella Fitzgerald/ Louis Armstrong version of Gershwin's "Summertime". You can listen to it on YouTube. I've heard many great artists present this atmospheric piece beautifully but the Ella/ Louis version, I believe, is the best. Mum is an Ella Fitzgerald fan and Grandad Bobby was a Louis Armstrong (Satchmo) fan so, for me, there is added significance to this version. It came out in the late fifties, around the time I was becoming aware of the power of music. I didn't realise that then of course. I was no little Mozart!

After the second war there was so much to smile about for a child growing up in Epworth and Belton with relatives and friends in the other Axholme villages. We loved our big skies and historic landscape, our rivers, dykes, drains and turbaries, our commons and copses and our productive farmland.

In the fifties the Isle of Axholme was playing catch-up with the nearby towns of Doncaster, Scunthorpe, Gainsborough and

Goole. Increased access to utilities meant pipes and cables were being put down and, in the summer months, the air was often heavy with the smell of tarmac as conduits were covered. I have a horrible memory of having a filling at the dentist's when he had taken over the doctor's surgery at the traffic lights in Epworth. Men were drilling the road at the same time the dentist was drilling my tooth!

The patchwork of summertime memories always seems to have a great deal of blue and yellow overall. It hardly ever rained of course, just as it always snowed in the winter! But when it did rain in those days it was of great significance, especially for the farmers. My birthday is in June and, as a small person, I felt it had to be bright and sunny. I think it usually was but one June birthday wasn't. I genuinely felt cheated. After all, it would be another year before my next birthday. As a gift, Grandma and Grandad Johnson would sometimes buy me a summer frock. I was duly grateful but I found them less interesting than the ones Mum made for me. Mum even made up the patterns sometimes. She had such flair with fabrics and often finished things off with embroidery. Grandma Johnson gave her a number of Uncle Neville's old shirts and from them she made shirts for Mike. She made a splendid winter coat for me from an old maternity coat she had. We rarely had machine-made cardigans or jumpers as Mum knits too. A very fond memory I have is of getting up in the morning to find my doll, Jane (named after my cousin), dressed in a complete new outfit. This happened twice. Once Mum had knitted her a jacket and bonnet in blue and made her a little blue and white dress from an old petticoat of mine with, underneath, a vest and knickers knitted in white. The other time she had a pink coat, bonnet and leggings with a pram blanket to match.

Until Dad went into business we were poor in monetary terms but I consider I was the luckiest little girl in the world. My teachers often told me how clever my mother was to make our clothes and they would admire the new ones as they came up. This made a little girl, who liked pretty things, very happy. We didn't wear a school uniform. In the summer the girls wore cotton dresses with a cardigan, ankle socks and crepe soled sandals. Maureen Whiteley was always the first of us to come to school in a summer frock and, as soon as she did, we begged our mums to let us wear ours. The response I received each year was "Cast ne'er a clout till May is out!" The boys generally wore shorts and short sleeved shirts, rarely T-shirts at that time, again with ankle socks and sandals. After the summer holidays clothing slowly took on a more sober appearance until we were wrapped up in woollens against the autumn frosts.

Summer was the time for freedom. Freedom to play down the lane, freedom to make dens in hedges and trees, freedom to create dubious potions, from wild flowers and herbs, to turn friends into... even more beautiful friends! Before glyphosates were used extensively to clear weeds, atrazine was experimented with but was found to have undesirable effects. This was at the time I was growing up and I remember the point when the lanes and hedgerows of Axholme were significantly diminished in terms of wild flowers. Thankfully they are glorious again now. I knew little of sci-fi then but, looking back, I think that time seemed strange and to be feared. So some memories were not in blue and yellow. One has to put the use of such chemicals into some kind of perspective however and it is true that farmers were positively encouraged to increase their yields by using them. We continued to "dig for victory" long after the war had ended.

When my brother, Mike, became interested in fishing, he was really quite young and his first rod was a twiggy branch, some string and a safety pin. This he used with no success except for the weed which he dredged up and examined carefully for signs of aquatic life. When he was equipped with more sophisticated fishing tackle he would take himself off to fish the River Torne, often with his friends. I never liked the fishing part but I loved just sitting on the bank amongst the wildflowers, watching the butterflies, dragonflies and damselflies and listening to the birdsong. I suppose I must have been a bit of a nuisance really.The River Torne has an interesting history and was one of the problems for Vermuyden when he began to drain Hatfield Chase. His first engineers appear to have made a mess of things and it took some time for matters to be put right. I think pike was the intended catch for Michael but I'm not sure how many succumbed to his lure!

When I started with hay fever as a child, I had no idea that it meant every June would proclaim prolonged sneezing, a tickly throat and red, itchy eyes. It wasn't going to keep me indoors for long though. The joy of summertime surpassed the miseries of hay fever. I have sometimes, in recent years, done the gardening wearing a dust mask but when I was younger I would tie a handkerchief around my nose and mouth, cowgirl-style. Whatever our condition, we couldn't wait to be allowed outside after we were dressed and breakfasted in the long summer holidays. When we were very small we stayed in the yard where Mum was able to keep an eye on us. She had a rug which she spread out for us to sit on and where we played with our toys. When the men came to empty the toilet pan it was easy to clear away our toys because there were not many of them. I'm not very fond of the "You don't know you're born!" philosophy but I can honestly say that not one of our toys was disregarded. Each one was quite special. There were times when we didn't play with toys but went to the Thurlow playground where there were two sizes of swings and what we called the zig-zag. It was a long bench, divided into seats, suspended from a metal frame and with standing spaces where two people could make the bench work to and fro, from the opposite ends, allowing those on the seats to have a ride. Of course restraint was required and sometimes the older kids were a little too enthusiastic. My little brother became a victim of the zig-zag when two big boys were working it and Mike was thrown from his seat, suffering a broken leg as a result. Poor little chap was in such pain and, later on, the itching under his plaster drove him crazy. The Thurlow holds many memories, not just of summers but of all seasons. In the summertime there was cricket and bowls and tennis. The cricket was serious stuff and should never be confused with a game of rounders! We kept well clear of the cricket ball. My Grandma and Grandad Johnson both loved their cricket as did Great-Grandad Charles Johnson and Great-Grandma Emma too. Yorkshire cricket can be traced back to the mid eighteenth century and their Yorkshire families were great enthusiasts. The bowls club at The Thurlow was close by the primary school. I was fascinated by the greenness of it. Those things are significant when you are small. As I grew a little bit older, I developed an interest in tennis. I was never a sporty person, always preferring to walk or cycle in the countryside for exercise, but I really enjoyed playing tennis. Later on, after primary school, I was disappointed that, because of my lack of proficiency in other areas of Games and P.E., I was never taken seriously in tennis and I really wasn't that bad at it! The tennis courts at The Thurlow were grass courts and I paid my half-crown and joined up there, enjoying every minute of playing and watching others play. My Grandma Johnson had been a local tennis champion in her younger days and she gave her beautiful Slazenger racquet to me. The old wooden and gut tennis racquets don't cut the mustard nowadays I'm afraid but I loved mine and always returned it to its press when I had finished playing.

Then there was The Show. Epworth and District Agricultural Society put on the event at The Thurlow for a number of years and it was so exciting. As school children, we were given a free ticket to get into the show and it was a major annual highlight for us. We were sure to bump into relatives and friends there, some of them we hadn't seen since the previous year's event. I loved the gymkhana and admired the horse/rider relationship. I was spellbound by the grace of it all and by the way the horses did the things which the humans wanted them to - usually. My very favourite thing though was the flower and produce tent. The miniature gardens were so magical that they might have been Hampton Court or Isola Bella. Cliffy Gravel's amazing models were wonderful. The patience and creativity which went into the making of them were beyond this little girl. I would stand and gaze at them until I was called away. When I was older and allowed more freedom, I would go back again to take another look. The canvas tents were always warm and had their own peculiar grassy smell. They also filled up very quickly when we had a sharp and sudden shower! The next day, after Epworth Show, Mike and I, when we were old enough, would go back to the Thurlow on our bikes and fill up our saddlebags with dozens of bottle tops from around the site of the beer tent. I loved their maltiness as we sorted out our booty into sets and proceeded to count them. There were rather too many and so we often gave up. It was a strange feeling to be back by the silent and eerie beer tent where the previous day there had been so much repartee, laughter and chinking of glasses.

Our bicycles meant a great deal to both of us. There was not as much fast traffic on the roads in those days and it seemed safer generally to be out in the big wide world. We got around the Isle easily apart from the odd minor mishap. When I was out of primary school I was allowed to venture a little further and I loved to whizz (somewhat irresponsibly) down Holgate (pronounced 'ogat) Hill and through Churchtown, Belton to visit Grandma and Grandad Temperton. Later on, when we moved to live near them, I would sometimes bike back into Epworth to the library or to the Youth Club which was held in the Alexander Kilham Memorial Chapel close by the traffic lights. Our bikes gave us freedom and a little independence. They were a stepping stone in our development. With the increasing popularity of international cycle races, there is a different view of cycling but, for me, a bicycle will always be a facilitator. One of our regular bike rides was part-way to Wroot through Carrside, Epworth. Our teachers sometimes took us on nature walks there but, on a bike, it was possible to go even further up the road. I had a favourite ash tree and the willows were a welcome sight. Some of them had partially hollow trunks and they offered shelter to small creatures along the length of the ditches and sometimes in hedgerows. Willow and alder are native to the Isle and still work well by drinking up the excess water from the field boundaries. I believe there to be around six different types of native willow and I'm not going to pretend to know which ones grow in the Isle of Axholme but I am certain that there is more than one type present.

Going towards Wroot from Battlegreen, Epworth, just after we had gone under the bridge and through the gap in the railway embankment, and turning to the left, we found, on our right, a remnant of poorly drained land. This was, back in the fifties and early sixties, an oasis of sedges, grasses and rushes including reedmace. Heavy rainfall would create a sump there. Yet there was something almost spiritual about it as if it were the last gasp of a native landscape before it too was adapted to suit our post-war requirements. It is easy to imagine Islonians harvesting the reeds and rushes there through bygone summers.

When I visited my grandparents at Rose Cottage, Belshaw Lane, Belton (Carrhouse) in the summer months, it was only on rare occasions that the door was closed. For a long time they had up, over the door opening, a heavy cotton curtain almost resembling deckchair fabric but, when the colourful strips of plastic labelled "fly-screens" became available, Granny and Grandad put up one of those instead. When the summer was ending and the cooler weather on its way, the screen came down and the door was closed again. Today we speak of garden rooms and patios as an extension of indoors but back then we had no garden rooms and no patios and yet the summer gave a freedom to adults and children alike. The door was open and life moved seamlessly between indoors and outdoors. Peas, for example, would be shelled while sitting out in a garden chair. Many were eaten. Who can resist the exquisite sweetness of a freshly picked pod of peas? At Rose Cottage, where I spent so many happy hours, summer meant lessons in growing things and harvesting them and deck chairs on the lawn with jugs of lemon barley water for the children. I had a favourite glass which had painted on it some children with black faces and white dresses .Amongst my memories are the strangest little things. Grandad Bobby would take me out to his vegetable garden to fetch a lettuce for tea and what I remember is how he used such an opportunity to thin out his lettuce row, enabling the plants which remained to develop further. There would be a few very pale leaves around the chosen lettuce and they would either pick up and grow or they would become green manure. I remember picking blackcurrants with Granny Ivy so that she could make blackcurrant jam. If you've never picked them you will not believe how many blackcurrants are needed to make a reasonable quantity of jam. And then the topping and tailing! Granny and Grandad had gooseberry bushes and gooseberry pie remains one of my favourites to this day. Every time I eat it I am transported back to those wonderful summers. I didn't much like picking them off the spiny bushes though. I have since discovered that a very few finely chopped mint leaves picked at the same time as the gooseberries actually enhance the flavour of a "guzzgob" pie. We all eat food from around the world now - and enjoy it. However, when I was a child, our family never did. One of our classic summertime meals was ham, new potatoes with mint and peas. Still a favourite with us but Mum used to pour the fat from the ham over the new potatoes and we are told now that we really shouldn't do that sort of thing! The peas had to be shelled. That was a job given to us to keep us out of mischief but we soon learned which were the sweetest ones to eat raw. The "boiling" was somewhat reduced in size. Dad always liked his potatoes steamed. Dad knew his spuds! You know, much negative comment is made about British cuisine but I don't think that is fair. For example, Granny Ivy's meat and potato pie was delicious and the combination of pig-fry and Yorkshire pudding was wonderful! Pig-fry was not generally eaten when there was no "r" in the month though. Perhaps the sudden influx of convenience foods to the supermarket shelves meant that the weary cook of the household breathed a sigh of relief and skills were lost for a time but I think they are being reclaimed now. Other favourite summer meals of mine included minted new potatoes, runner beans and sausage with Mum's delicious sausage gravy. By choice the sausage came from Hills' Bakery on Albion Hill in Epworth. Mr.and Mrs.Hill were experts in charcuterie as well as being excellent bakers. Once I was old enough to go "up street" on my own, I was given a little list to hand over to Mrs. Hill or another of the ladies serving in the shop ::

"12 links of sausage, 4 thickly-cut pork chops and 2 lightly-baked teacakes, please"

The list varied but there was always a "please". Dad liked Mrs. Hill's souse, made from the head of the pig and set in jelly. I pretended to like it. It was not so bad with plenty of vinegar and pepper! Dad enjoyed watching me share his favourite dishes.

If we saw renegade oats growing at the side of the road we used to pick them as you pick flowers. We kept our shiny sweetie wrappers, from Christmas and Easter, in a jar. Oats which were still green yet formed were ready to be pulled and to have their heads wrapped in the tiny pieces of pretty foil. Once a bunch of oats was finished they looked attractive standing in a vase until they gathered too much dust. They were notoriously difficult to dust as the fragments of foil would drop easily.

When Dad bought pea and bean crops, growing in the farmers' fields, and employed people to pull them and bag them ready for sale at the markets, I would go along with him and "help". The smell of the peas was singularly summery. It is something which remains with Lincolnshire summers although the giant pea harvesters have taken over from the gangs of workers now. The women who worked amongst the peas and beans were big-hearted, fun-loving folk and told jokes with language quite new to me! In the early sixties there was a joke being told on the pea fields of Lincolnshire about someone named Christine Keeler. I asked Dad to explain. He didn't!

There are a number of food references in this account because summer is the time of plenty. Most people still used age-old techniques to preserve food for the winter. A great deal of jam was made. Mum's old jamming pan now sits in my kitchen holding our eggs. That summer evening, when we walked along Battlegreen to get Mum's jam pan from a man who lived opposite Frank and Margaret Frankland, is quite clear in my memory. It was one of those evenings when there was absolutely no air movement. A classic balmy summer's night. Chutneys were also made for the winter, and pickles too. Some people preserved beans in layers of coarse salt. There was no waste. Cats, dogs and chickens were given any leftovers. We didn't know then, for example, that leftover bread and butter pudding might kill a dog due to the inclusion of dried fruit.

Living in Belton, after Epworth, was quite different. The few shops were quite a distance apart. The village was at one time known as the longest in England. I suppose that has changed now as many commuter villages are edged with great belts of ribbon development. Belton, perhaps out of necessity, divided up into smaller communities such as Churchtown, Carrhouse and Bracon, coming together at All Saints Church in Churchtown or at the Methodist Chapel on the High Street. Mum and Granny Ivy were members of the Mothers' Union and that meant being able to help at garden parties, fetes and bazaars. It also meant that I sometimes got to go along on trips with them. To prepare for the fund-raising events there was much to be done and the ladies met regularly in each other's homes to make items to sell. Mum must have knitted dozens of bobble hats, always striped and colourful. They were for the Christmas bazaar. All Saints Summer Garden Party used to be held in the grounds of the old rectory, a late 17th/early 18th century building. It was a perfect spot but, when they moved it to the new rectory garden, the summer sun beat down on us all. There was very little in the way of shade. I don't remember the "Bowling for a Pig" continuing in the new rectory grounds but I do remember Grandad Bobby and Mr. Picksley running it in the garden of the old rectory where there were trees and bushes. I remember the good old fashioned games too, including quoits. There were sometimes competitions for the schoolchildren, such as the butterfly painting competition where you were given a folded piece of paper and you thoughtfully, remembering a butterfly's balance, shook blobs of thick paint onto one half, closed up the paper and gently pressed the halves together, then opening it and, hopefully, revealing a spectacular butterfly. I must try that again sometime.

"Hill Top", down Belshaw Lane, was a favourite walk for us and I can remember the moment when Granny would untie her pinny and, having rolled it up, push it under the cushion. Granny was ready. Sometimes we had the Church magazines to deliver first. Those walks with Granny Ivy taught me much about the natural world around me. Granny sometimes had different names for plants and trees to those I had heard Mum or my teacher call them. Late summer meant blackberrying and we took with us enamel basins to fill with the sweet ripe fruit. They were combined with Bramley apples to make plate pies. Before using the berries they had to be spread out so that the tiny creatures, which had hitched a ride, had the opportunity to remove themselves.

A trip to the seaside was another highlight of summer. We made lots of happy memories on those days. As we drove towards Bridlington, we would all strike up with "Oh I do like to be beside the seaside, I do like to be beside the sea, Oh I do like to stroll along the prom prom prom, Where the brass band plays tiddly om pom pom..." and Granny was sure she could smell the sea. She had us all taking in great gulps of sea air. Grandad Bobby would make himself a sun hat from a handkerchief knotted at each corner and Granny would paddle with us. When we arrived home there was sand everywhere. It seemed to have crept into every little seam and curve. The sea had stolen the colour from our sandals and Mum applied polish upon polish to make them right again. But it was worth it!

No account of childhood summers would be complete without the mention of the frustration a small person feels at having to go to bed in daylight. Mike and I were unsettled by the light and sometimes the heat too. We dangled dangerously from bedroom windows and after we had been spotted and duly sent back to bed we would call out games to each other from our own beds. We played a form of I-Spy. Although we were in separate rooms we had to remember what was in the other's room and guess what it was which began with, say, B. Easy - that one!

The last mention in my account of summertime memories is of the voice of Jean Metcalfe who presented Family Favourites every Sunday lunchtime. We always listened to the programme and the combination of music and connectivity especially for those who couldn't share Sunday lunch (we called it dinner in those days) warmed the heart so that my memory of it is always with windows and door open, bright sunlight streaming in and the smell of roast beef and Yorkshire pud everywhere - whichever Axholme house we lived in. Dad had served as an RAF driver in Palestine after the war (his 18th birthday was 22nd October 1945) and he knew the importance of staying connected with home. I can't listen to Richard Rodgers' "With A Song In My Heart" without thinking back to what we always referred to as "Forces Favourites" - on a warm Sunday in summer.

Cornerstones

Whatever your politics, your religion, your background, you can't escape the current climate of uncertainty in Britain, Europe and beyond. Sometimes one is tempted to leave the radio off. We're not great television watchers in this house so, apart from online news, we are generally spared the illustrated version. But it isn't as bad as it seems, in that we've been here before and we are here to tell the tale. This isn't the first time in our history that we, the people, have felt unsure about the country's future - our future. The Isle of Axholme has had its share of unrest. The drainage years and their aftermath come to mind immediately but there have been other occasions, before and after, when Isle folk have struggled with their collective lot. A castle (Kinnard's at Owston Ferry) was built as fortification; tunnels (it is said between Low Melwood and Hirst Priory) were created for escape, and justice halls (eg Crowle) were meant to address problems of the day. There has never been a perfect era - at least not for all classes. However, the Islonians were able to focus, through centuries, on their churches and religious buildings. Standing tall and prominent across the wide open spaces of North Lincolnshire, they gave significance, not only to the landscape, but also to the spiritual lives of the people. Those people were not always as God-fearing as their masters would have liked but they had their beliefs, and the sight of these impressive buildings would provide the necessary affinity to a higher ideal to faithfully complete the daily round. Even now - in this age of SatNav - if someone asks for directions, it is quite likely that one will ask if they are familiar with the church and then give directions from there. Generally the largest and tallest building in the village, the church still acts as a lodestar.

Growing up in Epworth and Belton, I came to know Saint Andrew's and All Saints' very well. I was baptised at All Saints', Belton, as was my brother, Michael (even though we lived in Epworth when Mike was born), surrounded by our Temperton ancestors. While we were living in Epworth, as young children, we would occasionally go to Belton Church with our grandparents. Those were the days when a lady in Church without a hat was a peculiarity, the days when the heating was sparse and temperamental, and when almost everyone kneeled for prayers.

When we lived at Studcross Cottage, we attended the Baptist Sunday School on Station Road in Epworth. We were a mixed bunch of kids and we had fun as well as getting the religious instruction we actually went there for. We were still very much tied up with the land and so there was a lot of thankfulness in our gatherings. Another feature of Baptist Sunday School was the interest generated about children from other lands. We had happy parties too - spinning the plate was popular. There was a lot of good humour and many smiling faces.

We didn't start going to Saint Andrew's until we moved "up street" to Aston House. The Church Sunday School was a more formal affair and was held in the long building on Pashley Walk - where we also had ballet classes, on Tuesday evenings, run by Miss Credland. The hall had a background spiciness to it. I never understood why. Perhaps some wise person hid pomanders therein to counteract other smells! Each attendance gave us a picture to stick into a little book as a reminder of the theology of it all and also as evidence that we had turned up. We graduated from Sunday School to going to Church and joined the choir of Saint Andrew's. My naughty little brother did what naughty little brothers do and carved his name into the choir stalls. Mrs. Annie Ellison, who was a friend of my Grandma Johnson, was the organist, and Mr. Ellison sang in the choir with

Mr. Newborn and Mr. Hind. We had choir practice every week and sometimes sang at weddings too. Reverend Harvey was the incumbent and had been since 1955. When I was a child his sermons went over my head but he inspired me with his kindly manner.

I love this description by William Read, in his "History of the Isle of Axholme" (1858), of the setting of Saint Andrew's:

"From the Churchyard may be seen, northward, the Yorkshire Wolds, on the other side of the Humber, with the high grounds of Alkborough, and Burton Wood; eastward, Messingham and the town of Kirton-in-Lindsey; on the west, the distant hills of Derbyshire, the Church of Laughten-in-le-Morthen, and, in winter evenings, when night has thrown her dark mantle over the earth, the gaslights of Doncaster, and the blazing furnaces on the hills of the neighbourhood of Sheffield. Thus, from this single point, the view comprises a large portion of the country once covered by that ancient forest - the "Sylva Caledonia" of the Monk of Westminster - which sheltered the aboriginal Britons from the fury of their Roman invaders."

Epworth Church stood above the small town like a benevolent aunt, seeing all and being a constant marker and pointer. It has probably been so since the 12th century, but the first priest was recorded in the 13th century. Architecturally Saint Andrew's is an interesting building with masonry through different eras, particularly the 15th century. My great-great-grandparents, Thomas and Eliza Emerson, would have watched as the 1868 renovations exposed hidden gems within the church. George Emerson too, my great-great-great-grandfather, would have wondered at the skills involved in reflecting, through the restoration of the building, the High Church influence of the Oxford Movement, which was of great significance in the middle of the 19th century.

Mike and I, with the other choir members, put on our blue robes each Sunday - he with his brilliant white surplice and me with my little white pleated jabot - and slowly processed to the choir stalls. It is quite a long church and has points of interest throughout. My very favourite thing about it is the tiny stained-glass window at the end of the south aisle. I loved it as a child and I love it still. The glass depicts the Good Shepherd. I have seen lots of beautiful ecclesiastical buildings - when the children were young we used to visit as many English cathedrals as possible, and Saint Magnus in Kirkwall, Orkney, was our local cathedral for a number of years - but this image has stayed with me since I first entered Saint Andrew's as a little girl. I remember focussing on it when I attended Church with my mum on the Sunday after the Aberfan disaster in 1966. I wasn't in the choir on that day. Mum and I sat together quietly weeping for the 144 people who had died, most of them children. Sadly the Aberfan Disaster came to mind after the dreadful fire at Grenfell Tower on 14th June 2017. Warnings had been ignored and the frustrations of survivors, in seeking justice, developed into understandable anger.

The fabric of the religious buildings of our country - whether they be churches, chapels, mosques, gurdwaras or temples - are stone, bricks and mortar, steel, wood and glass. They can however speak to us, as does the image of the Good Shepherd in Saint Andrew's, by quietening the stresses of modern life and settling the mind on something which is not corruptible. Restoration of the fabric of our religious buildings has far reaching effects on local inhabitants (whether regular attenders or not) and visitors alike. Saint Andrew's has had a restoration project very recently and, if you google it, you will see excellent photographic coverage of the various stages.

I can remember sledging down from the church to Belton Road, where the garden centre now stands. This was before the existence of Castle Drive and even before there had been the excavations at Vinegarth in the mid-70s - way before that!

Other memories associated with Saint Andrew's include going with my Grandma Johnson to replace the flowers at the grave of her parents, Robert and Blanche Emerson, and her brother, Alfred Ernest, known to my mother as Uncle Dick. Earwigs are not my favourite insect and there was an abundance of them amongst the dead flowers so I stood clear as Grandma took them out. My job was to pass the new flowers - almost always cut from Grandad's garden - so that they might be placed as a tribute to my recent ancestors. Saint Andrew's Churchyard seemed to me an honest place - a place of quiet respect. Keith and I visit graveyards - some neater than others - across England and Scotland in our efforts to put more leaves on our family tree and, on each occasion, it has seemed an honour to be there. The greenness, the birdsong, and the signs of occupation by small animals give these places a sense of belonging to all time. They are not about decay and bones but rather cameoes of unfolding communities.

When I joined Epworth Youth Club it was in the days of hipsters and bell bottoms. Being trendy was a big thing, but we were way behind the kids from the nearby towns. By this time I was travelling daily on the bus to school and was incredulous at how the girls in my class would stay in bed until the afternoon at weekends and spend hours in each other's bedrooms experimenting with make-up and listening to records. This all came to the Isle eventually, but we were quite tied to the old country ways in the 60s. Early to bed/early to rise etc.. The Youth Club was in the Kilham Memorial Chapel which had previously been the Methodist New Connexion. It was close by the traffic lights and not far from the Wesley Memorial Church across the road. I have been inside the Wesley Memorial Church but not very often. What I remember about it is the care taken with every aspect of the interior. From outside it is an elegant late 19th century building but it was the interior which struck me. It was as if someone had polished every tiny part of the woodwork inside. Does someone still do that I wonder? It made me think of the famous statement in one of John Wesley's sermons that "Cleanliness is next to Godliness"! I remember the gardens as being lovely and have an image of a weeping cherry tree. Up the High Street a very little way stands the Temperance Hall where I went with Dad to insure my first car - a blue Ford Anglia. The "blue" bit was crucial! I knew nothing about the workings of motors but Dad taught me some of it. Nowadays, however, I haven't a hope! Technology is wonderful but there is only so much I can take in! In 1970 the NFU had their office in the Temperance Hall. I suppose it is quite natural that Epworth would put up its own Temperance building in the 19th century, with its strong connection to Methodism.

The first time I ever went to the cinema in Epworth was when Mum took me to the Rio to watch "Bambi". I loved it and couldn't wait to share it with my own children but my kids really don't like it at all! Later I went to see "The Young Ones", "Summer Holiday" and "Goldfinger" with friends. There were many others but I remember these ones particularly as I had graduated, at that time, to being allowed out independently. The cinema was on Queen Street. It was a building remarkable for its size and plainness. Sometimes we had to queue to get in and, if it had been raining, people would sit steaming in their horse hair seats until they had dried off! A lady would walk up and down the aisles with a flashlight beaming it into the faces of courting couples and others who were not concentrating on the film. There was a break for ice cream but, if you could resist the ices, you could take the money and buy a bag of chips on the way home instead.

Going to live in Belton and attending All Saints' Church seemed an easy progression and not at all awkward. I really did like Aston House, but Mum and Dad had planned and built Branscombe Lodge and it was next to Dad's business site so it was a natural move and, very important, near to my grandparents' cottage. Roly Ellis, who lived at West Butterwick and was married to the much older sister of my mum's friend, Margaret Saxon, had built our bungalow, laying the masonry in a style Mum had seen and liked from our annual holidays in Devon. He did the back wall first and it wasn't exactly what Mum wanted so, if ever you study Branscombe Lodge, you will notice that the side and front walls are a little bit different from the back wall. Trivia.

Instead of walking up an avenue of mature trees to arrive at Saint Andrew's Church in Epworth, Belton Church almost seemed to wriggle into its spot in Churchtown, and its place there was representative of the Christian sense that the Church is the people. It squeezed in amongst us as an anchor of security. I remember it as a place of light, outside and inside. I was confirmed there on 5th March, 1969 by the Bishop of Lincoln. I attended 8am Communion (rarely!), Morning Prayer, Holy Communion and Evensong. I wonder if they still have Evensong, many churches don't these days. Grandad Bobby was fond of Evensong and I have warm recollections of sitting by him, watching the sunlight fade outside the church. Occasionally he would move his leg a little to ease the discomfort he felt. Grandad had problems with his legs for all of his 83 years but I never once heard him complain. "Abide With Me" was his favourite hymn, and I can't hear it or sing it without thinking of him. Harvest Festival was a popular service and some people who worked the land would go to church then when they may not have gone at other times of the year. All Saints looked splendid bedecked with gathered corn and other produce. I loved to hear the church bells on a Sunday and also on practice-days. Belton had an excellent team of bell-ringers. Here, in the north of Scotland, we hear only the bidding bell so, when Keith and I were in York recently, I phoned the family so that they were able to listen to the music of the bells as they remembered them.

Next to the church was the Collinson Cooper Hall. The Mothers' Union and ladies of the parish thought themselves fortunate when it first opened. Everything was light, clean and new, and it must have been a pleasure to prepare strawberry cream teas there in the summertime. The hall has very recently been refurbished so a new group of parishioners will now enjoy its freshness.

Before the Collinson Cooper Hall was opened, we had events in the Public Hall. Brave folk would stand up and sing solos or give recitations. One of my favourite monologues was *The Lion and Albert* by Marriott Edgar which began:

There's a famous seaside place called Blackpool,

That's noted for fresh air and fun,

And Mr and Mrs Ramsbottom

Went there with young Albert, their son.

I also loved to hear songs such as "We'll Gather Lilacs" and "My Dearest Dear" - it is rare that anyone recognises them today, but I sometimes listen to them and I'm happy to say that one of my daughters enjoys listening to them with me. My appreciation of opera was kindled by the Victorian and Edwardian Ballads and Light Opera pieces which were chosen to entertain us at the Public Hall in Belton over half a century ago.

After the evening's entertainment and refreshment, the younger members of the audience clattered across the wooden floorboards as parents and grandparents critically summarised the evening with friends and acquaintances. "Well I know I couldn't stand up there and do that!"

I attended Epworth County Primary School and I covered that in an earlier chapter, *Elementary Education*. I did spend time at the old school in Belton too - as that was where the Cub Scouts met every Monday evening and, along with Dr. Jane Mitchell and Janice Tindale, I helped to run the meetings for a while. I was Bagheera. We were normally in the school hall but sometimes we took the boys to the swimming pool at North Axholme School in Crowle. Occasionally we met at Dr. Mitchell's house, on the High Street, to light fires in the garden and cook horrible sausages and "dampers". Of course it was fun but I hope those lads - no girls allowed in those days - are not now satisfied with such risky cuisine. As far as I am aware nobody was affected by salmonella infection but we were literally playing with fire. Belton Church of England Primary School was also where I did my second teaching practice. (The first was in Guisborough, North Yorkshire and the third was in Scunthorpe.) At that time Miss Mary Housham was the Head Teacher. It was a friendly school and I have fond memories of the lovely children. My parents, aunties and uncle, grandfather and great-aunts and great-uncles had also received their education there.

These buildings were all significant as part of my early life in the Isle but there were other structures too which had meaning - such as disused railway bridges, the Epworth Market Cross, and the War Memorial at Grey Green, Belton.

Everyday Life In The Slower Lane

The pace at which we live our lives today seems relentless. Blink and you miss that important anniversary or an opportunity to meet up with friends. We all have our theories and philosophies about how we reached this whirlwind way of life but, whatever they are, it is a fact that our living was done at a slower pace in the middle of the twentieth century. To begin with, not everyone had a car. The two-car family was virtually unheard of. I was in double figures before we had hot water without boiling a kettle. Imagine me watching steamy water come out of a tap when I went to school. I was so taken with it that, when sent to wash up jam jars which had been used for painting, I let the hot water run and run until the glass cracked. I was scared and mentally scarred for life! Lots of us ate up the previous day's left-overs for breakfast, had a cooked dinner in the middle of the day, and wine was just for Christmas. When I arrived home from hospital as a child, I gave accounts of crispy golden cornflakes with milk and sugar. I must have been a bit of a pain really. My parents probably thought I might have stayed there a bit longer! We have come on a lot since those days - some of the changes have been good, some not so good.

At Studcross, we had our milk delivered by Mrs. Skinner, who wore a headscarf and fingerless gloves in the winter. She would pick up Mum's milk-checks - plastic coin-like discs - count them and replace them with the same number of glass bottles full of milk which still had the cream on the top. The colour of the milk-checks denoted the type of milk required. Mrs. Skinner took away the empties too. Mum was very particular about her empties - they had to sparkle! We had full-cream pasteurised milk, but Granny Ivy had sterilised milk. The bottle was a different shape with a thin neck and a metal lid which needed a bottle opener, like a beer bottle. Mum's pasteurised milk had a foil top which was loosened by pushing down on the centre with your thumb. Granny's near neighbour, Mrs. Eva Needham, had her milk left with Granny's by Granny's gate at Rose Cottage. Mrs. Needham would come to collect it and would sometimes pop in for a natter. Granny found out quite a bit of local intelligence that way. However, she mainly just kept on working - preparing dinner, baking, ironing, dusting or maybe washing a few things out in the sink. She would sometimes call back to Mrs. Needham from the scullery but, as the years went by, Mrs. Needham grew more and more deaf so Granny had to remain closer in order to make her hear. If the old lady didn't catch what had been said, the response would be "E?" as in egg. It is funny how things like that stick in your memory. The people who lived down Belshaw Lane, were so important to us. They were part of the fabric of our own lives. Mrs. Needham lived with her husband, Fred, who had served with the Royal Engineers in the First World War, on the lane to Northferry Farm, the home of the Beecroft family. Fred, who was of my grandfather's generation, married Eva in 1951, the year before my own parents were married. The Hackneys owned the other side of the lane and had a tempting swing in a tree at the end of their property. I think it was a horse chestnut as I remember conkers in autumn.

    How simple were our daily lives back then? We didn't know how simple they were. Some things, with the help of technology, have, ironically, almost returned to an earlier time though. For example, my mum never made her own bread as her grandmothers did but, because I have a machine to do it for me, I weigh out my flour and produce, at the touch of a button, sufficient for lunch and pack-ups on a daily basis. Labour-saving devices in the kitchen mean that we are able to produce high quality meals without the effort required by previous generations. Back in the mid-50s and 60s, we bought our bread from Stamp's Bakery, where Pashley Walk joins Chapel Street, or from Hill's Bakery, on Albion Hill, both in Epworth. The great sliced loaf increased in popularity and it was possible to buy one, wrapped in waxed paper - and, later, plastic bags - from almost any grocer in the Isle. When the prices, as well as the loaves, seemed to be rising quickly, the old folk would say, "Aye, it won't be long afore tha'll need a ten bob note to pay for a loaf!" A ten shilling note - now there's a memory! Of course, when we were sent to either Stamp's or Hill's to buy fresh bread, the glorious smells which emanated from the kitchens and the appeal of the recently made pastries and cakes as well as the bread products all on display were almost too much. Neither shop was very large - Stamp's was especially tiny - and sometimes we had to join a long queue outside in order to get to the counter. It wasn't like queueing in a supermarket, people actually held conversations with those they knew instead of assessing the products on the conveyor belt in front. We can know so much about fellow shoppers today. I am mildly amused at the concern regarding privacy on social media - which one opts into - when very personal information is on view each time one shops at the supermarket!

Queues were in evidence at Barnes and Breeze's every Friday afternoon too. Isle folk lined up to wait for their copy of The Epworth Bells when it was hot off the press. When we were at Epworth County Primary School we had a school trip to look around the printing works across the road from Barnes and Breeze's shop. We were given metal printing plates with our names on them. We learned about type-setting and other processes involved in producing the much-loved local newspaper.

Epworth is still a busy township. The shops may not be the same but it is still quite lively. My Grandad Johnson lived, for a while as a young child, in one of the houses on the High Street terrace where, when I was a little girl, Mr. Hudson had a sweet shop. On that same terrace was Mr. Spencer's paint and wallpaper shop where he also took in shoes which needed mending. Across the road was another sweet shop - owned by Mrs. Wardle - where I sometimes bought sherbet fountains and liquorice pipes with hundreds and thousands on top of the pipe bowl. In summer, Mrs Wardle also sold banana lollies, partly covered in milk chocolate. Going quite a way down High Street, past the traffic lights and towards Battlegreen, was Mrs. Coggan's shop where I bought my pineapple chunks for 3d. Amazing how many tempting sweet sellers there were - and that I still have my teeth!

Sometimes Mum would go to a wooden hut in Battlegreen, not far from Mrs. Coggan's, where they sold all things pork-related. I think Mr. Barlow and his two sisters prepared and sold the meat. Their brawn was highly regarded. There were other butchers in Epworth too. Hills, on Albion Hill, were pork butchers as well as bakers and Mr. Geary had a butcher's shop at the top end of the High Street. (Mrs. Geary was the well-respected "Guillemot" who encouraged our interest in nature study.) On the same side as Mr. Geary's shop was a fish and chip shop (fish and chips were sold in newspaper in those days) and a grocery shop, with Sinclairs running a shoe shop next to Mr. and Mrs. Hind's house. My dad, who was in the same line of business as Alec Hind, used to tell me that Mr. Hind was unlikely to be a really successful businessman because of his kindly nature. Mr. Hind sang in Saint Andrew's Church Choir at the same time as me and he truly was a kind man. The Maxfield family had another butcher's shop next to the Post Office further down the High Street. There was also a van which went round Epworth delivering meat. Roland Miller and his wife, Lilac, sold meat from their shop down Westgate in Belton and had a van too. Pidds were butchers in Crowle and had been since way back in the nineteenth century. So we did alright for protein in those days! We had a bit of a pattern to our family's meat menu - Sunday was a roast, Monday was a stew made from the left-over roast, Tuesday was pig-fry or ham in summer, Wednesday and Thursday were either oven-cooked steak, lamb chops or pork chops and Friday was sausage day. We didn't usually have meat on a Saturday - we had fish and chips instead. There were three fish and chip shops in Epworth then - Johnsons, Camps, and the one mentioned above.

Mr Cliff Trimingham and his wife, Edna, ran the grocery shop next to the Alexander Kilham Memorial Chapel. There was a tiny shop in Battlegreen, run by Mrs. Naylor, which sold basic items but Mr. Trimingham's was my mum's go-to grocer. She used to take a small red notebook into the shop once a week and Mr. Trimingham would select all of the items on Mum's weekly list, box them and deliver them in his little van. Granny Ivy, down Belshaw Lane in Belton, used to do the same with her weekly list, but she shopped with the Co-op. When I was on holiday from school, I was often there when the weekly grocery box arrived and I loved to see Grandad Bobby's eyes light up when he spotted his pipe tobacco on the top. The grandfather in the fairytale film, *Parent Trap*, was said to smell of peppermint and pipe tobacco - well so did *my* grandad! He loved his extra strong mints and he would offer them to me from when I was quite young. Granny said they were too strong for me but Grandad would grin when I coped well with them. Mum also shopped at the Co-op for other things as they sold fabric and reels of cotton in their drapery department and Mum was always sewing. Sometimes I was sent to shop there and to this day I can remember Mum's divvy (dividend) number - 25151. Later on, the Co-op gave out stamps before the present system of annual rewards came in.

Mum knitted too, and Mr. Trimingham's sister-in-law, Mrs. Percy Trimingham, ran the wool shop on the High Street. I learned to knit and had used the new chunky wool, called triple-knitting, to knit myself a jumper before I left primary school. This wool was something quite new. Until this point the thickest wool was double knitting and, generally, it was considered that the thinner the wool the better the finished garment. That was all very well but, for a youngster who kept stopping to see how much her creation was growing, the preferred 4 ply, 3 ply and 2 ply didn't give the required results! I chose to knit in thick wool for a while - until I learned more patience. Going up the step into Mrs.Trimingham's shop was so exciting. There were rows of bagged wool in different colours and different textures. Patons and Baldwins, merging with J.P.Coats in the early sixties, brought out a range which represented aspects of the countryside with tiny flecks in earthy colours. I found some in a charity shop about eight years ago - full balls with a partly knitted garment thrown in - and I have since knitted myself a cardigan with it. The quality of the wool is superb. My Auntie Gwen had a shoe and drapery shop on the High Street in Crowle and she also sold wool. Her Robin wools were exciting too - such as a green and cream twisted together and a golden yellow with silvery white flecks. I bought my wool from Auntie Gwen too and of course I had longer to make up my mind at Auntie Gwen's. She gave - not just family but all of her customers - sufficient time to consider before making a purchase, sometimes letting people take things home to think about it. Sandra Colenutt, later Everatt, worked in the shop. Sandra was patient too.

Before Auntie Gwen, had her shoe and drapery shop in Crowle, she had a tiny shoe shop just up the road. I think there is a Chinese take-away there now. Auntie Gwen and her husband, Pete Jackson, served Crowle well for many years.

There were those two shops and also their taxi service and involvement in the church as well as the local football teams, so both she and Uncle Pete will remain in the memories of many Crowle folk for years to come.

The Isle of Axholme had quite a variety of shops. Auntie Gwen started in retail by working for Mr. and Mrs. York on Albion Hill, Epworth. One of her jobs was to take a suitcase round the Isle to sell drapery to those who were unable to get into the shop. The Yorks were across the road from Hills bakery and pork butcher. I remember the shop as being very deep and going back into darkness. I suppose that is because I was small. They sold furniture as well drapery, and it was easy for a child to feel lost amongst sofas and sideboards and seating.

In Belton the shops were spaced out throughout the village. There was no cluster of retailers. A fish and chip shop was on the High Street across the road from Siddaways, and another one - run by Mr. and Mrs. Maw - was on Westgate, not too far from Grey Green Corner. The butcher was way down Westgate; the Post Office was at Grey Green opposite the War Memorial; Ann Glew, the hairdresser, was down Bracon; Raymond Kenyon had a grocery shop on the High Street and Mrs. Shapland ran a shop that seemed to sell a little bit of everything in Churchtown. By the time we moved back to Belton, I was travelling in to school each day on the bus, so I left my bike in Mrs. Shapland's yard after having biked, satchel on my back, from Carrhouse. The shop was at the top of Stocks Hill and the bus stop was at the bottom - across the road from Mr. and Mrs. Bean's bungalow. (The older Mr. Bean lived in a house at the edge of the fields behind the Steers Arms, not far from the old road. Old Mr. Bean, who had been a coach painter, was quite famous locally as he lived to be 101.) When we arrived at the bus stop each evening after school I would catch a glimpse of the tea tray elegantly set out in the living room of the younger Mr. Bean's bungalow. The

Bean family were all long-lived and respected in Belton. Mrs. Bean, from The Crown Inn in Churchtown, used to play the organ in All Saints' Church.

We had a dentist and a doctor too, of course. Mr. Talbott was the dentist by the church in Epworth. Mum went there but I had the school dentist until I left primary school when I went to Mr. Traynor. He operated from Dr. Macgregor's tiny surgery at the traffic lights in Epworth and later I went to Mr. Traynor's surgery in Thorne. Before Dr. Mitchell came to the Isle, Dr. Macgregor, who lived on Burnham Road in Epworth, managed Epworth, Belton and the surrounding hamlets single-handedly. Dr. Macgregor died in 1964, aged 57. Little wonder he died early when you think about his workload. Later Dr. Mitchell, who made his home with Dr. Jane on Belton High Street, was to develop the practice further and, before I started teaching, I did a spell with him as a receptionist at the new surgery by the Post Office in Epworth. The Drs. Mitchell were very fond of Grandad Bobby, who gardened for them and became a friend to their three boys, Robert, Anthony and David. Home visits were general in those days. People expected them and the doctor expected to set aside a sizeable stretch of time each day to perform them. I had two spells in hospital when I was a child and one of them was in the isolation hospital in Scunthorpe after I had contracted scarlet fever. Our little hearts ached when we were only able to see our families occasionally and through glass. The nurses were kind but they were not our mums. When I was in the isolation hospital I had a kaleidoscope which I really loved, but it couldn't be sterilized to bring home with me. I have loved kaleidoscopes all my life and have forced them on my children who, in turn, have sometimes given kaleidoscopes to me as presents. My newest one is a kaleidoscope, given for Christmas by my husband, which can be used with or without artificial background illumination. Kaleidoscopes were patented exactly 200 years ago. Who knew? I certainly didn't until I very recently researched their history and found that they were invented by a Scot named David Brewster. I had always thought until then that they were of German origin.

Schooldays were quite different back then, not least in the way we were walked to school by our mums and never driven to the school gate in a car. There weren't that many cars about at all. There were garages to mend vehicles and also for petrol. If there was nobody around, you would peep your horn and someone would come from the nearby house ready to serve you at the pump. No self-service back then. Mr. Matthews had a garage at the top of Church Street in Epworth and it was possible to buy most vehicle-related things from there. People used to have a go at sorting out problems with their own vehicles but, now that so much is computerised, it is quite a different kettle of fish.

As we grew a bit, we were allowed to walk to school by ourselves, and the kids who lived on the far edges of the villages sometimes biked in. Many people rode pushbikes in those days - not the sporty ones you see everywhere now but often the old "sit up and beg" type. My Grandad Johnson's, a "Rudge", has travelled all the way from North Lincolnshire to Northern Scotland with me. It sits in our shed waiting for the day when I get around to weather proofing it so that it can go on display and withstand the vagaries of our Scottish weather.

There were a few racers about when I was little but they were very swanky! Men and women had quite distinctively different bikes. Men had a cross-bar, and a man's bike was generally heavier than a woman's bike. Because there was no cross-bar, a lady was able to set off by scootering a little way and then delicately getting on the seat as the bike gathered speed. It was a throw-back to the days when a lady rode a horse side-saddle. Sometimes her bike seat was made more comfortable by stretching an old knitted hat over it and finishing it off with a plastic rain hood to keep it dry should it be left out in the rain. Men were often seen riding their bikes with sacks of vegetables on their handlebars, or sacks of something lighter - or maybe canvas field bags - across their backs. Into the field bag would go the lunch tin, which may or may not have been for an actual packed lunch - lunch was sometimes a second breakfast (wrapped in greaseproof paper) with workers biking home for their mid-day dinner. Not unreasonable when you remember that in those days more calories were needed to keep these human machines going - work was often physically harder and homes were always colder.

How did we keep warm? Some may have had central heating but my family didn't. Even when we moved to Aston House we kept warm with a coal fire in each of the front rooms - we didn't often use them both at the same time though – and, of a winter's morning, the Esse range in the kitchen was lovely to come downstairs to, and it gave us our hot water. Jack Frost never managed to paint the kitchen windows at Aston House! We burned coal on our fires. Nowadays many people burn wood and, where we live in Caithness, quite a few burn peat, but generally people have central heating whether they have a stove or not. There were several coal merchants in the Isle when I was growing up and their coal varied from delivery to delivery. I remember dusty coal which smoked, coal which spat out little pieces onto the hearthrug, slatey coal, coal which was in such big lumps it had to be broken up and coal which was in such small pieces that the air couldn't get through it to create a flame - unless one lifted the resulting mass with a poker to allow the air to get underneath. Isle coal merchants included Harrisons of Epworth, Cayleys of Belton and Hobsons of Crowle.

We were warm and well-fed. We took exercise without realising. We were well cared for by the medical profession. Our pleasures were simple and our relationships were based on mutual respect and trust. The pace of everyday living in the middle of the twentieth century was not so relentless but I wonder which of us would go back? One car per family? Frost patterns on bedroom windows in winter? No mobile phones? No internet? Even drinking to the bottom of your cup and getting a mouth full of tea leaves? We each make our own assessment. Our theories and philosophies are, thankfully, all that little bit different.

No Farmers, No Food, No Future.

The Industrial Revolution is a clanging bell in the subconscious of British people. Images of those forced to move into towns and cities, to live in squalor and work until they collapsed, will never equate to the horrors of the slave trade, our ancestors had little choice but to move from their familiar homes in the villages and countryside of Britain to the dark and overcrowded towns which instilled fear and bred disease. James Temperton, the younger brother of my great-great-grandfather, John (1829-1895), took his young family from Belton to Honley, near Holmfirth, in West Yorkshire and worked as an agricultural labourer there, finding employment for his children in the cotton mills. His son, Thomas, became a wire drawer and was the father of Miss Nellie Temperton, born in Mirfield and known to many as a music teacher in Epworth. Thomas and his wife, Annie, formerly Annie Crabtree from Belton, are buried together in Epworth. So that particular family returned to its roots. Not everyone was able to do that.

In Scotland, the clearances forced many abroad or to eke out a living close to cliff edges, where they sometimes had to tie up their animals and children to stop them from blowing over. Badbea in Caithness is one such clearance village and I challenge you to visit it without feeling an overwhelming sense of despair. Many people say they get that on visiting Culloden and I do too, but Badbea gives me the same feeling - the little person, in spite of his or her beliefs, passions and devotion, is disposable to those with power. Sheep replaced the cottages and gardens of the straths in Scotland. In England, generations would pine for their country roots whilst working machines in monstrous, impersonal factories.

The Agrarian Revolution meant the availability of seed drills, attributed to Jethro Tull but, in fact, around in a more primitive form since biblical times, and a more general and increasing knowledge of crop rotation. I stayed with a school friend in Messingham in 1965 and her grandfather, a farmer, took us out to the fields where he sowed his crop from a basket, scattering handsful of seed over the soil. That is something which has stayed with me whenever we sing "We plough the fields and scatter" at harvest time. However, the 18th century was the time for enclosure, and the end to much of the strip farming which had been in operation for many centuries. The new farming practices were welcomed by the landowners. Who benefited? They did.

Before the drainage, Isle land was generally unsuitable for arable farming. There were some areas, such as Mill Hill in Crowle, where crops had been grown for many centuries before Vermuyden, but these were on the scarce high spots and were cultivated in strips. We managed to hold on to our strip farming in the Isle of Axholme and there is still evidence of that agricultural landscape to this day in Epworth and near Haxey.

In the mid-nineteenth century, Charles Darwin addressed the question of selective breeding, although work had been done with sheep and cattle in the eighteenth century. Farming kept up with the times. In the period when my great-grandparents were born, much was being done to convert pasture to arable land and to reclaim fenland in order to grow more crops which would feed the increasing populations of the towns and cities of Britain. In the twentieth century, the First World War changed the agricultural landscape again. Men were across the water, fighting and dying for something they barely understood, and women were becoming involved in the running of industry and agriculture. In The Epworth Bells, 24th March, 1917, women were being recruited for work on the land:

" . . . . As the women will be doing men's work, it is of the utmost importance that they should be of good constitution and vigorous. [That's me out then!!] Thousands of strong healthy women are required at once, and all who realise the national importance of working to increase the food supply should apply for terms and conditions to the nearest Post Office, Employment Exchange, or National Service Offices, where enrolment forms may be obtained."

Farmers in Axholme have succeeded in adapting their methods and crops over the years. For example, when I was growing up in Epworth and Belton in the 50s and 60s, sugar beet was grown locally and taken to the sugar-beet factories of Lincolnshire to be processed. Sugar beet seemed to me to be a long-standing local crop but I have since discovered that it was not grown in Britain on a large scale until after the First World War - the war having created a shortage in the supply of sugar. As a little girl, living in Studcross Cottage with my parents and my brother, I was very taken with the shiny green leaves of the sugar beet crop growing in the field next door. They seemed to be the last word in greenness - unlike the red-veined beetroot leaves which my grandfathers grew in their gardens. Whole fields of beetroot, or red beet, could also be seen in the Isle of Axholme. In the 26th May, 1917 copy of The Epworth Bells, Mr. George Cooper of Haxey is credited with having successfully experimented with beet manuring using Crimson Red Globe - a deep red beet, slow to bolt and still popular today.

The sugar beet factory at Brigg closed in 1991, so I was surprised to find that British-grown sugar beet is still responsible for 50% of our sugar. Sugar beet is generally sown in March and harvested in October, although crops have been left in the ground as late as the new year - a bit risky though. Singling of beet, where the weaker plants were taken out, was done in June - wearing a hat against the sun (common sense) - but the consequences of not wearing hats had proved fatal on more than one occasion. Hoeing continued through July.

When it was time for the beet harvest, and beets and mangold wurzels were being taken along the roads - particularly the bumpy lanes of the Isle - it was wise to give them a wide berth. When one dropped, it went with quite a thud. A cart-load of mangolds is a pleasing sight in the autumn - the mangolds make a warm yellow/red glow behind the tractor - a bit like a gaping medieval hearth full of glowing embers. Mangolds were cut in November and clamped or "put in a pie". The pies were made with straw and mud, the mud pie top being left off until the crop had finished breathing. Sometimes they were stored in a loose straw-covered pile against the shed or byre where the cattle were kept in the winter. Beet and mangold wurzels - same family - are just one example of how we think that our history is forever-history when, in fact, our farming past and present is rich and varied, constantly changing to meet demands. Although Elizabethans ate beetroot, it is unlikely that the people of the Isle grew them so early but it may be that, during the reign of Charles I, they made an entrance into the kitchen gardens of Lincolnshire by way of the Dutch, who were ahead of us when it came to beet production - and engineering. Vermuyden, when he drained Hatfield Chase, brought to the Isle a great deal of his native Dutch culture - not all received magnanimously

Celery also grows well on the soil of Axholme, and it is said that the Lord Mayor waits to have his show in London until the celery is ready for harvesting in the fields of Haxey. On 6th January, 1917, a plea for celery appeared in The Epworth Bells:

"As the Isle of Axholme is so famous for its celery, may we earnestly beg that ALL growers will spare us a little from their abundance. Everyone must surely realise the great debt of gratitude we owe to the Navy. It is mainly to their unceasing watchfulness that we in the Isle have celery or anything else to call our own. We need scarcely tell you again how keenly these gifts are appreciated by the sailors themselves. We should be grateful for all gifts to be sent to Epworth by mid-day on Thursday next."

Uncle Peter Temperton, who farmed at Wroot Grange, regularly shared a head or two of celery with us in the winter months. I have never since tasted any celery which came close to that. I can see him now, placing the celery, wrapped in newspaper, on the kitchen table then going to stand in front of our open fire and steaming. The gents wore woollen trousers in those days and when it was wet or foggy outside, they took some drying off. My son, a bit of an expert in outdoorsiness, tells me that Merino wool has a great waterproofing quality to it - well I can tell you, from my memory, that the woollen trousers worn by men in the 50s were almost certainly not Merino!

According to a book published in 1538, carrots have been grown in Britain for even longer than beet and celery. Dad started his farm produce business by washing and packing carrots with Walter Law in Mr. Law's shed. This was close to his home between the chemist's shop and the King's Head Inn on Church Street in Epworth. Dad later washed carrots down Belshaw Lane in Belton, on land which had belonged to the Temperton family years before. As you go from Belton down towards Belshaw, on the right hand side of Belshaw Lane, it was just past the tiny bungalow where Auntie Rose (born Annie Rose Florence Mary Temperton, 1906) lived, with her husband, Uncle Billy Clark, at the time of her death in 1965. After a while Dad built up the potato-packing side of his business and worked from buildings behind Mrs. Franks' farm which I now know, half a century later, as Crosshill Farm. It was just Mrs.

Franks' to me but Crosshill Farm has an interesting ring to it and, if I were the new owners, I would be skimming old documents for mentions of it. I think maybe they are already on with that, and I wish them every success.

The potato harvest was at the time of the October half-term and my parents and grandparents had many a tale to tell about those Indian summers when they themselves were children and worked in the potato fields of the Isle. There are less pleasant tales too - of mud and cold appendages. They worked to help buy their new winter coats. There's a thought. The potatoes were put into a clamp but we called them "pies". When the pies were opened - no, the birds didn't begin to sing - the small mammals and amphibians came out of hibernation. They were often disorientated so it was best to wear wellies or high boots!

Potatoes still suffer from blight, and today's techniques for managing it are similar to historic methods. Sarpo Mira is a maincrop potato which is classed as blight free but many varieties cannot make such a claim and it can take only days from onset to a total ruination of the entire crop. Spraying as a preventative has long been held as an answer to this problem and, a hundred years ago, in March 1917, farmers were encouraged to order their sulphate of copper at a price not exceeding sixpence halfpenny per pound (Epworth Bells).

Dad was not washing carrots or potatoes in the summer months and it was then that he bought crops of peas and broad beans and employed people to harvest them, sending the produce to the big wholesale markets in towns and cities such as Manchester. Peas and beans were cultivated after the drainage and some varieties were used as animal feed. Peas and beans take nitrogen from the air and fix it in the soil so when crop rotation took off with Turnip Townshend in the eighteenth century, it followed that the use of clover as a nitrogen fixer would extend to the cultivation of peas and beans too. Clover had been grown in the field on which my parents built their bungalow and so the garden which was subsequently planted there really flourished.

One bean which was growing in the Isle of Axholme, before the beans with which we are familiar today, was the bog bean. Bog beans grow in fenland, in bogs and in marshes. Forsinard in Sutherland is the ideal place for them to grow, but it used to be so in the Isle too. They have a bitter taste and have been used for centuries as a herbal cure for gout and arthritis, but caution is recommended as very few studies have satisfactorily proved the use of bog beans to have positive effects and, in fact, their use can upset the digestive system.

On a recent visit to the Isle, I noticed that Crowle still has its pasture on Wharf Road and it makes a charming entrance to the little town. Isle pastureland has diminished now but cattle were kept in all of the villages and townships from the River Idle in the south to Garthorpe in the north. Uncle Peter kept them at Wroot Grange and I was in awe of the very early mornings this entailed - every single day of the year. I love early mornings but that was hard and never-ending work. It still goes on of course - modern technology means there is plenty of up-to-date equipment but someone has to operate it on dairy farms up and down the country.

In the days before I was born, many people kept their own pig and sometimes kept a pig for another person, sharing the cost and sharing the meat. This happened less and less in the 50s but there were people who were able to farm pigs in fair numbers. Mr. Coggan, who lived at the Studcross end of Battlegreen with his wife and daughter, Pat, had a number of pigs which delighted me as a small child. The little ones fascinated me but the big ones could be a bit grumpy. There was also a pig farm, again not far from Studcross, down

Carrside, Epworth where there was some housing for the men who worked there.

My Temperton ancestors worked the land in Belton in the nineteenth century. Reuben Temperton (1791-1870), married to Elizabeth Mitchell from Crowle, was an agricultural labourer all his adult life except on the 1861 census when he was described as a line dealer - so whether he grew flax and sold it, or he just bought and sold it, I cannot tell. Reuben's son, John, my great-great-grandfather - married to Hannah Watkinson from Ferry - was an agricultural labourer in 1851. He is recorded as a blacksmith at his son's baptism in 1855 and an agricultural labourer in 1861 and in 1871. In 1881 he was a small farmer of 4 acres but in 1891 he is recorded as being an agricultural labourer again.

On Mum's side, Thomas Emerson (1789-1853), married to Mary Gleading from Auckley and my 4th great-grandfather, was a farmer in Epworth. Their son, George (my 3rd great-grandfather), was a shoemaker on the 1841 and 1891 censuses, a flax dealer in 1851, later becoming a farmer after his father's death. In the census of 1861 he was recorded as a farmer and a line merchant. In 1871 he was a flax dresser (breaking, scutching and heckling the flax) and ten years later he was recorded as an agricultural labourer.

Although flax and hemp were grown in the Isle in the medieval period, it was in the nineteenth century that big strides were made in their production, enabling some local growers and dealers to benefit from the success of the oil and the fibres. Some Victorian buildings still standing in Crowle are a testimony to this. The dainty blue flax flower must have been a common delight in days gone by - as it says in The Epworth Bells, 21st July 1917 :

"Outside Ireland flax is a crop unknown in the British Isles, and though the fine flower was a familiar sight in days gone by, few people of the present day would recognise it in the fields. The causes which have led to this result are numerous, but not insuperable, and when the necessity is so great the burden is laid on the country to overcome it."

Now I often find the delicate plant included in mixtures of wildflower seeds. It is a gentle reminder of my ancestral roots!

Wildflowers along the edges of fields and at the sides of roads and lanes in the Isle are again a pleasure to view but, for a time, they were missing from around the villages. Aggressive use of herbicides and the uprooting of hedgerows left a sorry and sometimes desolate picture. Farmers, previously persuaded to pay fantastic sums of money to chemical manufacturers, are now keen to work alongside nature to improve their crops and yields. This is such a positive step towards the good management of our countryside, and towards our better mental and physical health.

Harvest Festivals are in full sway at the time of writing. Some churches have had them already but some don't take place until November. Saying "thank you" is fundamental in the farmer's year and, when I was growing up, many farmers who did not usually attend church were seen, with their families, in the pews at harvest time. The time to gather in the crops is exhausting for agricultural workers - even with modern machinery - not least because of the rush to beat the weather. In August 2017, I stayed in Eastoft, in the north of the Isle, and enjoyed the talk, in the local, about the urgency to finish the harvesting of this field or that field before the expected rain. When I was young, a thunderstorm could flatten a field of corn and render it useless to the farmer. Today, corn has been developed to withstand most beatings and remain harvest-ready. I noticed, on social media, that there was some rain at the Festival of the Plough (17th Sept., 2017). A shame, but a pertinent reminder of how those who work on the land will always rely so much on the right weather so that the crops and animals thrive, and so that the workers can complete each task in its season. Cereals are emblematic of harvest but, at school, we were encouraged to also consider coal - which was then mined not far away in South Yorkshire - as well as the fish which were landed at Grimsby. Here, in Caithness, we have a "Tatties and Herrin'" service, remembering that the south bank of Wick owes its existence to the "silver darlings".

I would like to tell you that I used to ride in the wagon when the golden corn was being led homeward. What a lovely tale that would be. The truth is I did it just once. My memory of that ride is swaying into Greengate, Epworth and wondering if I would stay put! There is something about the fragrance of ripe corn which is difficult to describe but it snuggles one down soundly into the cornucopia of goodness. The warm weather in late summer is well received before the cold and damp of the months to come, reminding me of the small child who watched out of her little bedroom window, on such a balmy evening, as the harvesters worked the reaper binder across the mere. Combine harvesters have changed all that. They have also eliminated the need for the threshing machine and I have no doubt that farmers bless the day the combine harvester was invented. My first acquaintance with a combine harvester was when Dad took me down the Wroot road to see Uncle Peter operating one. It seemed to me that he was so far away up there and that this monster-machine had incredible power. They are even bigger and more powerful today and have, themselves, come to typify harvest time. The floors and ceilings in the price of corn have long been established, for about 200 years to my knowledge, and not without opposition. A hundred years ago, in January 1917, prices were fixed for wheat and oats:

Wheat, 60 shillings per quarter of 504 lbs
Oats,　38 shillings and 6d per quarter of 336 lbs

Later in that year, harvest labour had become a problem :
11th August, 1917, The Epworth Bells

"Mr. Tong reported that soldiers were being now sent to Lincoln Barracks and that 450 would be available at the end of the week for harvest labour. Mr. Tong also stated that it was now possible to obtain the release of any particular soldier desired provided he is in one of the lower categories and not in training for overseas. It was absolutely impossible to obtain the release of any man now on active service overseas."

A week later, the Epworth Bells states that a start had been made with the corn harvest but the poor weather had meant little progress had been possible up to that time.

In the 13th October, 1917 copy there are accounts of Harvest Festivals across the Isle including one at the Wesleyan Church in Crowle and a summary of the subsequent meeting on the Monday evening which:

" . . . was addressed by the Rev. S. Pickard and Mr. W. R. Harrison, and after the service, Mr. J.J. Cranidge kindly sold the gifts of fruit, etc. The proceeds of most successful services amounted to £19/3/7, to be devoted to trust and circuit funds."

The following week gave an account of the services in Epworth Parish Church where the text in the morning had been Jeremiah vii verse 20 :

"The harvest is past, the summer is ended, and we are not yet saved."

I wonder what our ancestors thought of that - after all their hard work, their dreaded and dreadful telegrams, their collective fear for the future?

After the corn harvest fruit trees in Isle gardens again deliver their bounty - just as they did in 1917 and for centuries before that. I wonder how many people are able to keep apples in storage as my Grandad Bobby did. There is something almost magical about eating a stored apple, with its slightly wrinkled skin, in the colder months of the year, which keeps one firmly in touch with the big picture. The seeds are still in there.

The end of the harvest is a time for reflection - and a time to look once more at the old ways - customs, beliefs and sayings. Time to remember what they meant to a child growing up in the mid-twentieth century Isle of Axholme.

Whether Weal Or Woe

Piles of crunchy brown, yellow and orange leaves have collected in front of and behind our house. When the wind blows, they shift and settle in a different place. When it rains they become slippery and present a hazard on the paths. The midges have been hanging around too. In Axholme it was the Men o' Wroot which were the *bêtes noires*. When they were particularly bothersome, Grandad called them little blighters. (He never came any closer to swearing within my hearing. Men didn't swear in front of women and children, and women never swore - not the ones I grew up with.) The Men o' Wroot were at their most dastardly through harvest time - tiny creatures rampaging over any part of the anatomy left uncovered. When they had ceased to pester us, we would be reminded of them through the winter months each time we looked at a photograph or a picture in a frame - there they were peppering the image until someone had the time and inclination to separate the glass and wipe them away. The conditions in the Isle of Axholme were perfect for their success. The irritation they caused, however, was shorter lived than the goitres which were believed to have been the result of imbibing the Axholme waters. They don't go away with the cooler weather.

At this time of the year, in mid-twentieth century Axholme, my two grandmothers had changed their summer window curtains for their winter curtains. Their summer curtains were lightweight and let the sun through in the early morning, but the winter ones were heavy and resisted on the rail when closed against the chill evenings. They not only stopped the light but they also helped keep out the cold and the draughts of winter. Door curtains would have been put back in place by now. As kids we used to hide behind them, imagining we were invisible, but small children find it almost impossible to keep still and, after a few pointed questions and lures, we would appear:

Granny: I wonder where Susan is. Oh well, I will have to find someone else to give this to.

Out comes one curious Susan from behind the door curtain.

And, thinking of doors, who amongst us would ever go into a house through the front door and out through the back - or vice versa? Only the thunder bolt could do that with impunity. In a thunder storm it was required that there should be a point of entry and a point of exit for any force which may attack the home. Superstition was very much in evidence amongst the older folk when I was growing up in mid-twentieth century Lincolnshire. It was still believed by many that it was bad luck to leave a person's house by way of the opposite door to the one through which you had gained entry. That was not a problem when visiting my Grandad Bobby and Granny Ivy as they only had the one door. The imagery relating to doors is plentiful and the entrance to a person's home and castle may say a great deal about that person, but the welcome from within is everything. Much later, when we lived in Crowle with the first four of our six children, our neighbour, Mrs. Dowson - a few years younger than my grandma - told me how her mother gave her this advice when she was about to be married:

"Keep a clean doorstep and a clean apron and don't natter over the wall."

After that conversation, I naturally took the brush and removed the cobwebs from around the door, noticing, for the first time, the children's muddy fingerprints on the glass.

Granny Ivy used to change her apron when the washing-up was completed after the midday meal. We called this meal dinner in those days as it was the main meal of the day back then. My own aprons were chosen for the big front pockets as my kids were in construction - working for that great engineer,

Sir Lego McAlpine - and their baby siblings had to be protected from the small, red and yellow masonry. They seemed to be able to find the brightly coloured choking hazards with the efficiency of bloodhounds. It didn't take long for my pockets to fill up.

As for nattering over the wall, that is what Mrs. Dowson and I were doing when she told me of her mother's advice. Guilty!

We had winter clothes and summer clothes when I was a little girl. I just didn't wear jumpers in summer, and I never wore sandals and short socks in winter. "*Cast ne'er a clout till May be out*" governed the actual day when our wardrobes changed. As soon as plenty of May blossom had been spotted in the hedgerows, away went the woollies and out came the cottons with cardigans folded neatly in the drawer for cooler days. It was always a bit touch-and-go at first and many thought it wiser to wait until the month of June. Mum, for example, was very wary of taking that giant leap forward into summer. We usually persuaded her to let us "go into" our summer things a little in advance of 1st June. But only a little. We certainly never admitted to feeling a bit chilly on the morning walk to school when the temperature had dropped overnight in late Spring.

At Easter, it was traditional to wear something new. In some places it was the superstition that should a person wear nothing new they would suffer ill luck until the following Easter - by which time he/she should have learned a lesson! I never heard it said in the Isle that bad luck would befall such a person. Perhaps we realised that not everyone was able to afford a new garment. It is true though that some people still liked to wear a new summer coat or hat to Church on Easter morning. Ladies don't often wear hats in Church nowadays, but I believe Easter Sunday may prove the exception and children in school or in Sunday school are still asked to design an Easter bonnet - perhaps for a competition. Prizes are invariably Easter eggs. The idea of wearing something new is tied in with the new life in evidence all around at Eastertide. I imagine my ancestors, with little money to spare, buying a yard or two of pretty ribbon in order to give new life to a bonnet that had seen better days.

The Easter eggs, which now appear on the supermarket shelves not long after Christmas, cannot possibly be received with more joy than those eggs given to Mike and me when we were little. One year Grandma and Grandad Johnson gave us eggs with our names written in icing. It may be quite common now but in those days it was really special. Another year Granny Ivy and Grandad Bobby gave me a little round basket with a chocolate egg inside and a plastic flower on the lid. Sometimes I think the pity is not that many children are given an obscene number of chocolate eggs at Easter but that the delight in the giving is reduced by the expectation. Hens' eggs too were significant, and I suppose they were even more important for babies in the days before processed baby foods. I have fond memories of Grandad Bobby insisting that our first child was ready for a soft-boiled egg when he was about four months old. Grandad called it a chucky egg.

The latest date that Easter will fall is the 25th April and so pork would still be acceptable - by five days - to mark the celebrations. Pig-fry, a mix of chopped pork, onions, liver and kidney, was never eaten from May through to August. Only when September came, and there was an R in the month again, was pig-fry served for dinner - often with Yorkshire puddings. At the same time hearth fires would be lit across the Isle, going out again briefly should there be an Indian Summer. I learned only recently that, for good weather in the autumn to be labelled an Indian Summer, there needs to have been a frost first.

Mum has told me how, when she was expecting me, Granny Ivy didn't want her to stay when Granny and Mrs. Picksley were processing a freshly slaughtered animal. It was considered to be bad luck but, as with many superstitions, there is some wisdom in it. Consider, for example, the risk from toxoplasmosis to the baby developing in the womb. Transmission from the mother to the fetus may lead to brain abnormality in the child or might even cause miscarriage. So, yet another old wives' tale with credibility.

In the Jewish religion, it is considered bad luck for women to attend funerals when they are pregnant. My Irish auntie (married to Grandma Johnson's youngest brother, Walter Emerson) told us that women didn't go to Christian burials in Ireland. In India, pregnant women do not shop for their babies until they have been safely delivered. Here in Scotland, we have seen the introduction of the Baby Box which forms a first crib with mattress, mattress protector and fitted sheet. It includes clothes from newborn to six months, a digital ear thermometer, a bath towel, changing mat and books. The Baby Box is entirely free to babies born in Scotland and I think it is a wonderful contribution to the level of respect and consideration which is shown by most to mothers and babies of all backgrounds. When I was a little girl, prams were never bought until after Baby had been born. Those beautiful coach-built prams, which are now associated with the Royal Family, were still the height of fashion for walking out with the newest family member back in mid-twentieth century Axholme. There were some stunning models available in the early 60s. We knew three sisters who had their babies at more or less the same times and they each had a magnificent pram - one had a grey/green colour, another had a white pram with a cameo type design of flowers on the chassis and a deep pink hood and apron, and the other sister had a bottle green pram for her two children. I remember feeling very sorry for twin babies as, when both hoods were up, it must have been terribly dark in there. Mr. and Mrs. Maxfield (the butchers) had twins but, before they were born, I have a recollection of their sister sitting out in her single pram in the garden next to Pashley Walk on Burnham Road. You couldn't miss babies in their prams then - their transport was almost as big as a bubble car! And those beautiful fringed canopies - how fabulous were they?

The "churching" of women after giving birth is almost unheard of but, when I was a child, it was still available to new mothers. In Judaism, women are considered unclean after childbirth but the "churching" of Christian women is concerned with thanking God for having survived the birth - even if the child was stillborn. There is no ritual purification involved - the ceremony is, instead, a blessing on the mother. I know, from accounts I have heard, that the generations in the Isle were often divided on this one by the 1950s.

Christenings were very much as they are today, but without the boozy party which seems often - but not always - to follow the service nowadays. Nothing wrong with a wee dram to wet the baby's head - as long as we don't forget the baby!

Babies have always been the subjects of customs and superstitions. One custom we followed in the Isle all the time I was growing up - and even when my own children were small - was blessing the baby by leaving silver underneath the pillow. Its purpose was to ensure that the baby would never be poor and I wonder if it may be linked with the gifts given to the Infant Jesus by the Magi.

We are heading towards Hallowe'en as I write this and we make quite a thing of it now but, in truth, little was done to mark the date when I was growing up. I don't know whether that was my own family's take on it or whether it was general but I have no recollection of anything happening at school either. Now Mischief Night, on the fourth of November, was another matter. We were little horrors then - knocking on doors and running away, and taking gates off their hinges. Yes, it was me!

In fact we did all the things you might expect now at Hallowe'en if you don't offer a treat when challenged at the door.

In the calendar year, Hallowe'en was the last of the three days for magic - May Day and Midsummer Night preceding it. I have heard it said that a hawthorn growing on its own should be avoided on those days and should not be interfered with at all on any day of the year - for fear of angering the fairies. Other days had powerful forces attached to them too:

" . . . the vicar of Owston, in the Isle of Axholme, reported that, in his parish, girls pulled three tufts of grass (the ranker the better) from a grave on the south side of the churchyard at midnight on St. Mark's Eve, 24th April, and laid them under their pillows, hopeful of the usual vision, repeating three times:

The Eve of St. Mark by prediction is blest,
Set therefore my hopes and my fears all to rest;
Let me know my fate, whether weal or woe,
Whether my rank is to be high or low.
Whether to live single or to be a bride,
And the destiny my star doth provide.

To experience no dream meant single misery."

(from DISCOVERING THE FOLKLORE OF PLANTS by MARGARET BAKER)

I wonder how many more similar verses meant something credible to our Axholme ancestors. I hope they are still out there somewhere - waiting to be recorded. There's a PhD in there somewhere. Anyone?

Both of my grandmothers knew the meanings of flowers - such as "rosemary for remembrance" and "thyme for thrift" - at least I always thought it was thyme for thrift but I have recently found that thyme also represents courage. Depends which publication you read or who you speak to. Granny Ivy and Grandad Bobby had roses (for love) growing on Rose Cottage. Not surprising. Wisteria and jasmine are lovely, dripping and draping around the entrance to a property. Wisteria for adventure and jasmine for wealth. Some plants, however, were to be appreciated from afar. The old folk took these meanings very seriously - larkspur for fickleness and poppies for death were best avoided. I have to say, though, that a drift of poppies in the border pleases me - both for their warm shades and the delightful fragility of the petals. Blue larkspur too is a favourite but it refuses to flourish in my garden. I enjoy the striking purplish shades in other gardens though. Throughout my life I have loved wild roses - and I see them still in Northern Scotland - but I also remember them blooming alongside elder flowers in the Isle of my childhood. The combination is exquisite simplicity – bounty too, as both plants are useful to us. The wild rose has a number of meanings, and simplicity is only one of them.

My great-grandmother (Blanche Emerson, Epworth) had a favourite shamrock, descendants of which have passed through the family since she died in 1955. My Auntie Shirley (Shirley Doreen Atherton, née Johnson) has some growing in her garden in Northamptonshire and I have some growing in our garden in Caithness. Shamrock is meant to keep snakes out of the garden and is also meant to represent, with its three parts, faith, hope and love. If you are lucky enough to find one with a fourth part - that is where the good luck comes in - although I reckon that if you have faith, hope and love, you probably don't need to rely on luck!

In the Fens - and I always think of the Isle being the northernmost reach of fenland in England - a holly tree was believed to prevent sorcery and so holly wood was used for door sills and handles. Holly was used, in the past, to make spoons and, if you are lucky, you can sometimes come across an old butter stamp made from holly too. Trees were respected by everyone. In this age of technological revolution many of us are hoping to re-engage the younger generations with an appreciation of the countryside and trees. People used to believe the trees which were so much a part of their everyday lives had spirits of their own and some trees were feared by country folk. The elder was known as the Judas tree and, many years ago when people were still afraid and superstitious, a hedger would feel obliged to apologise to it should he need to cut it down. After the Battle of Dunbar (1650) between the Scottish Covenanters and the English Parliamentarians under Oliver Cromwell, the surviving Scots were sent off to work as far away as the Caribbean but some were marched down to Lincolnshire to work as part of the drainage gangs. These men stayed in cottages which they felt were open to witchcraft, so they set about surrounding the cottages with holly twigs to make hedges. These hedges are still in evidence in a number of places and other hedges have some of their spiky descendants in amongst a variety of trees and shrubs. While I have been researching our family history, I have come across, in marriage indexes etc. a number of names which may have morphed from Scottish names and even some which are clearly Scottish. For example, in 1814, James Campbell married Hannah Brook in Epworth and, in 1836, Ann Mackenzie married William Carr in Crowle. These two Scottish surnames are one-offs in their index so James and Ann may have come south much later than the prisoners from Dunbar but I have Mitchells and Andersons in my tree and each of these names may be either English or Scottish. (We do have more recent Scots on our branches too.) An interesting thing about these two surnames for us is that they are on the same branch as the Cowlams who owned land, on Eastoft Moors, which was drained late in the eighteenth century. As I am compelled to check and adjust my knowledge, I become more and more delighted in the links I find with individuals and places - sometimes including other cultures - which I never knew I had.

I can't think of the ways and customs of the Isle without remembering Haxey Hood. Now a nationally famous game for Twelfth Night, it is believed to have originated in the 14th century when Lady de Mowbray rewarded thirteen farm labourers, who retrieved her errant silk riding hood, with thirteen acres of land - on condition that they re-enact the struggle to catch the hood each year thereafter. Read, in his *History of the Isle of Axholme* refers to the game as "Throwing the Hood" and adds, in a footnote, that:

"... *this rustic amusement is only observed at Epworth and Haxey. The inhabitants of Belton have occasionally practised the game as pastime.*"

I never knew of it taking place in Epworth though. In Orkney there is a similar event known as the Ba'. This takes place on Christmas Day and New Year's Day and, on each of the days, there is a Men's Ba' and a Boys' Ba'. Belton has its own fun though. Each year, from the early 1950s, energetic people ran around the village - and it is a very long village - taking turns to push and be pushed in a wheelbarrow. In 1972 I didn't want to miss the fun so I drove back from college in Ripon and got home just in time. There was a great deal of beer around back in the old days - much of it went wide though! As I remember, each competitor was meant to drink at every pub but, after a quick swig, much of the amber liquid went over the head to cool off. I haven't seen Belton Barrow Race since it was restarted just a few years ago but it is something I will look out for should we be down in summer. Great fun - to watch!

Epworth Fair was something we looked forward to twice each year. It was held in a field just off Albion Hill - behind Hill's bakery. Although it was visibly tucked away you couldn't miss it - follow the smell of oil and fried onions and the sound of very loud music. I remember Nelson Eddy singing "At the Balalaika", Ned Miller singing "From a Jack to a King" and Mark Wynter's "Venus in Blue Jeans". These songs will always be associated with Epworth Fair for me. As well as the fair in springtime, there was also one at the back end of the year. The main attraction then was either the speedway or the dodgem cars. I don't think they brought both at the same time. Mike and I won a couple of goldfish one year and we kept them in a bowl in the old washhouse, later described as a utility room, attached to Aston House until one winter morning we found them frozen solid. Poor things. Mum buried them but I always wondered if they would have thawed out - and lived - especially after "Adam Adamant" was transmitted on the television!

The Fair was early in May, and then again around the time of Michaelmas. These are close to ancient holidays and also, it is worth noting that, on May 8th, the villagers in Helston, Cornwall dance through their village to mark the day the Archangel Michael escaped the devil in France entering Britain by way of Cornwall. The devil threw a lump of granite after Michael but missed him, and the stone can still be seen in Helston. Now, I am seeing a link here with William of Lindholme who was supposed to have been in league with demons. It was believed that the doors to fairyland are open at that time of year and babies should be watched carefully in case the fairies try to take them away. No really - haven't you ever wondered whether your baby has been swapped? Our second daughter was a perfect angel - until she started crawling - then it was a case of going from the sublime into fairyland and back again!

Michaelmas is a Quarter Day, and a time for hiring workers. This meant that it was also a time for partying after the business of finding a job was done, tying in with holding the fair at that time of the year.

As well as Owston Ferry, Wroot had an ancient celebration of its own. Wroot Feast, commemorating Saint Pancras, to whom Wroot Church is dedicated, still brings much jollity, in July, to this small settlement on the edge of the Isle. I went there myself when I was a child and marched along the road with the other children. The legend of William of Lindholme holds that the giant was left by his parents while they went to Wroot Feast. William was meant to shoo away the sparrows from the crops but he "had a paddy" (tantrum) and threw a huge stone after them. It went off course so he followed his parents to Wroot Feast. He told them that he had imprisoned the sparrows in the barn. When the family got back they found most of the birds were, in fact, dead. Local farmers tried to move the stone but couldn't, losing several horses in their efforts. This led to a superstition that large stones found in the area should be left *in situ* and never meddled with.

Epworth Show is in August, and the Festival of the Plough - in Burnham - takes place in September. Although farmers are busy then, I think it is a poignant link with the old Harvest Home, when farmers and workers were equal and celebrated together, each toasting the other. I wonder if anyone keeps a corn dolly anymore? This was made from the last sheaf of corn to be cut and was a talisman for the next farming year as it held the spirit of the corn. I tried making one. It was unrecognisable.

Some things are lost but not all. The connection with the land continues even for those who are not directly involved in farming. Most people in the Isle have a garden, some have allotments, and everyone knows someone who likes to grow things. Growing plants from seed or nurturing young plants which someone else has started off is such a worthwhile thing to do. For those who are unable, unwilling, or don't have the time to actually grow things, there is always the opportunity to use someone else's produce - or food found growing in the countryside - to make preserves or wine. That connection with the soil helps to keep us in touch with our heritage. Most people made jam when I was a girl and there were competitions at shows etc. to make the best jar of jam. The Mothers' Unions and the Women's Institutes encouraged these endeavours, and there could be a bit of jam envy involved.

Christmas has a chapter to itself but, for now, a word about New Year. We observed New Year with extended family but there was no pattern to it, and people didn't drink heavily. It wasn't until we came to live in Scotland that I realised it was necessary to have a full bottle of single malt to hand at New Year and that you opened the door to all comers - whatever the hour. If you don't answer a knock at the door on Hallowe'en, you should be prepared for mischief but, if you have the lights on and you don't answer the door at Hogmanay, well, that is just not neighbourly! In the Isle of Axholme, a New Year's Day visitor brought a lump of coal or a small gift for the home but in Scotland the token tends to be liquid and taken from the same bottle as everyone else around.

The Christian celebrations of Christmas and Easter are observed in the Isle by most people, but some other Christian observances and ceremonies which happened in the past have become less popular now. When I was young, Rogationtide was still observed. The edge of the parish was toured by the priest and a blessing was asked for the crops. This was dwindling in interest back then but I am aware that, in recent years, some of the old ways have been picked up again so it would be good to hear that there is a renewed appetite for this. Rogationtide was an opportunity to focus minds on the natural world.

I wonder if the chapel anniversaries still take place. As well as the trailers going around the villages with happy children singing hymns and songs, there were also events in the chapels and in the halls. These events were not just attended by chapel folk but by church people too and by some who went to neither chapel nor church. Some hold their hands up in horror now at these formal events structured around biblical theology, but I wonder - when I think back to the pleasant faces in the cheerful congregation - was it really so bad? It is true that some adults were guilty of indoctrination but most led by good example. And those simple pleasures? Were they really that simple when they brought together villagers who valued the achievements of their children and young people? Those youngsters are my generation and I, for one, remember the way the faces of the grown-ups were illuminated by the various efforts of my contemporaries in taking part.

Life in Axholme was beginning to alter. We had started to branch out in line with the social change across the country, but the old ways are the roots which are there to steady us should things become more than a little frantic. And we do seem to be, as a nation, a little confused at present. "Blumin ummer!" as Grandad Bobby would say. I found "blumin ummer" in a glossary of Yorkshire words but, in the Isle of Axholme, I think you might say we are a curious mix of Lincolnshire, Nottinghamshire and Yorkshire - with a number of other influences thrown in - just love it!

A Funny Lot. A Lot of Fun.

Miriam Karlin was a left-wing campaigner and star of *The Rag Trade*, with other television and film credit strings to her bow. *The Rag Trade* - a series of amusing situations set in a clothing factory - while sharp and funny, was also an indicator that the workplace was changing in early-60s Britain. No more bullying by management - the workers were well placed to reverse roles! Karlin's strident voice and sense of employment justice appealed to those who felt themselves on the cusp of liberation but also entertained others with an ongoing sense of place in the established workforce of these islands. Them and us. One was able to laugh at the stuffy employer *and* at the touchy employee with a growing sense of empowerment.

The country was changing rapidly and it wouldn't be long before the old places of work disappeared in favour of concrete block-built factories and offices with rows of regular rectangular windows. Fortunately, some of the old places were left untouched until inspired architects converted them into apartments. However, many were demolished. The 60s was a time for levelling - removing examples of Britain's historic architecture and replacing them with very little of lasting value. It was the same with occupations. Many skilled craftsmen and women were no longer able to make ends meet when mass produced items became available across the country. This started to happen much earlier than the 1960s though. Lace making, for example, had become mechanised by the end of the 19th century, with handmade lace still being made in a few places such as Branscombe, Devon. I mention Branscombe specifically for two reasons - it was a favourite place of both my parents and they called our bungalow on Belshaw Lane, Belton,

"Branscombe Lodge" as a remembrance of happy family holidays spent there. The other point about Branscombe is that Honiton Lace - still famous - was actually made in Branscombe and only shipped from Honiton.

I have found examples of women making lace in Lincolnshire in earlier centuries. It is certain that groups of Huguenots settled in and near Sandtoft - some in Belton and some in Hatfield - in the 17th century, and they brought their skills with them. They were famous for their lace and, with a ready supply of flax in the Isle of Axholme, they were likely to have benefited the local economy as lace made from flax was considered a superior type and was much in demand across Europe. The Huguenots didn't stay for long in the Isle but there are surnames which suggest intermarriage. There were other jobs based on textiles and raw materials from the Isle. These too suffered with the advanced machinery which, in some areas, the Luddites attempted to eliminate. I wonder how many milliners, shoemakers, dressmakers, tailors, saddlers and harness makers or straw bonnet makers there are in Axholme today. I don't think I could have been a Luddite in the early 19th century - I see nothing positive in destruction - yet I have sympathy for their fears and insecurities. There are still people who feel as the Luddites did - but now it is computers and modern technology they are opposed to. Again, it is usually fear which causes their frustration and anxiety and sometimes anger. Granny Ivy's genealogy on her father's side was from the Wolds villages of East Yorkshire. The men had been tailors for generations until 1918 when the last tailor amongst them died. Granny's father, James Hudson, lived in Belton at the time of his death and had never attempted to follow his forebears in the occupation but died a retired labourer in 1941. Perhaps he saw the mass-produced clothing, which became available in the twentieth century, as a reason to find alternative employment.

He was described as a scholar on the 1881 census for Bainton when he was 15 years old - quite unusual. Many had left school, to find employment, well before that.

I'm a bit of a junkie when it comes to auctions. I'm in recovery at present because our house of curiosities is at capacity, and common sense must prevail. I just love handling old things. I can't bear to think that they may ever be discarded. I am most interested in the day to day items which few people seem to want and, if I don't buy them, they may end up in the skip. So I *have* to bid on them! The point I am getting to is that I bought a very old clock a few years ago and it worked for a short while. When it stopped working I had a go at fixing it - big mistake! After that, it was left at the local jeweller's - several times. In the end he stopped charging me as it seemed there was nothing which would *keep* it going. So I bought another old clock in a sorry state of repair with the intention of taking both clocks to a clock mender and going back a little later to pick up one composite working model. But there don't seem to be any willing clock menders anywhere near here and the kind jeweller has since retired. I wonder if my clock gave him the final nudge. My contingency plan is to try Inverness - 106 miles south!

Barry Guest ran a shop and workshop on Epworth High Street for a number of years and was trusted and respected in the Isle. This was before we all had digital clocks. Your clock or watch stopped functioning. Who were you going to call? Barry Guest. He never failed to cure his patients! Children who were lucky enough to be taken to his shop were full of wonder at the intricate nature of the job. The Isle always had someone who was able to investigate and repair a broken clock. A century earlier, in 1858, J. Woodcock of Crowle is recorded as the clock and watchmaker for the area. When Barry Guest was no longer able to mend our timepieces, I believe there was someone in Keadby who would take on the project.

Another craftsman, Watson Markham, my great-great-great-grandfather, lived a very long life and was always a boot and shoe maker through to a master cordwainer, mainly in Belton. Who, on the Isle, makes shoes today? Watson Markham, the great-grandfather of my Grandma Johnson (née Florence Mabel Emerson) would have seen the advent of factory-made footwear before his death in 1897 and, a little over ten years after that, glued shoes became an alternative to stitched ones. Another craft diminished. However, when I was a little girl, Mr. Spencer took in shoes, which needed cobbling, at his premises - a wallpaper and decorating shop on Epworth High Street. So people were still buying shoes of sufficiently high quality to bother taking them to be mended.

My parents' wedding photograph was taken on 19th July, 1952. It might be interesting to take a look at what people were doing then so I have listed everyone on the picture from left to right and, below the list, I will explain a little of what these people did in terms of occupation.

Charles Fenwick Johnson 1882-1956
Reuben George Robert Cecil Temperton 1900-1983
Ivy Elizabeth Temperton 1907-1993
Peter Temperton 1924-1994
Gwendoline Mary Temperton 1932-2017
Reuben George Temperton 1927-1986
June Margaret Temperton (née Johnson) born 1931
Robert Emerson 1879-1954
Shirley Doreen Johnson born 1934
Blanche Florence Emerson 1876-1955
Emma Johnson 1885-1962
William Neville Johnson born 1940
Florence Mabel Johnson 1911-1986
William Henry Johnson 1907-1979

Grandad Bobby (Reuben George Robert Cecil Temperton) was a gardener. He had problems with his legs which meant he was unable to join his brothers, Joe and Alf, in the army during the First World War. Grandad worked in the gardens of a number of local people over the years and he helped on the farms when an extra hand was needed. When I was a little girl he worked for Doctor MacGregor who lived near the traffic lights on Burnham Road in Epworth. Dr. MacGregor also owned a terraced cottage, across the road from his house, where Grandad did a lot of his potting etc.. I was sometimes allowed to call to see Grandad at work and I would admire the grape vine which grew there. I learned a great deal from Grandad about how to nurture plants. He had incredible patience. It seems to me that if someone is comfortable working in the garden then patience and a wonderful sense of calm becomes a part of the whole experience.

Uncle Peter Temperton was Dad's best man at the wedding, and he farmed at Wroot Grange, going to bed early in order to rise fresh for the milking before breakfast. The Tempertons were quite tied to the land - sometimes farmers, agricultural workers/labourers, gardeners and, in my father's case, a farm produce merchant. Dad was known as George but was named Reuben George Temperton and had other occupations before he became a potato salesman. He was a bus driver, a lorry driver, and sometimes a taxi driver. There is a theme here and when Dad was in the R.A.F. he was a driver there too. Dad took the bull by the horns and, in the early 60s, set up his own business as a farm produce merchant. Potato merchants were not a new breed in the mid-twentieth century. In 1858 there were potato merchants in West Butterwick (Michael Hall), Epworth (Thomas Bramhill and Peter Wressel), Garthorpe (John Tock) and Owston Ferry (John Clark and William Holmes). Life changed dramatically for us once Dad was established in business. We needed a telephone. Our first telephone number was Epworth 456. I can also remember Auntie Gwen's first phone number: Crowle 414. Not difficult. We have lived at our present address since 2009 and I still have difficulty remembering our home phone number. Annual holidays became possible - although they had to be taken between potatoes/carrots and peas/beans which was awkward when I had progressed from primary to secondary education, as they coincided with the exam period. Another huge plus for us when Dad's business became secure was that Mike and I were given brand new Raleigh bikes - after I had learned to ride on a second-hand bike which had belonged to Josie Bradley, a couple of years older than me, from Coronation Crescent, Epworth. The "Fruit Trades Journal", for growers and traders of fruit and vegetables, often with a picture of a blue labelled Fyffes banana on the front, was delivered weekly and, although I would read almost anything, I stopped at that - for a child it was about as interesting as putting away the decorations after Christmas! So growing things and providing produce seems general in the history of the Tempertons and goes back way. For example, Reuben Temperton, my great-great-great-grandfather was an agricultural labourer and died a relatively poor flax dealer in 1870. We have lots of Reubens (my cousin has carried this on, naming his son James Reuben).

Charles Fenwick Johnson started his working life as a railway tele clerk in Yorkshire. Charles was serving as a clerk at Epworth Station by the time the passenger service was opened in 1905, moving on to become the station master at Haldenby, Luddington with Garthorpe. He was promoted to station master for Haxey Town Station and, after another twelve years, also for Haxey Junction. By the time of his retirement in 1947, Charles had been employed by the LMS Railway Company for 50 years. My grandfather, William Henry Johnson, was the second son of

Charles and Emma and was also employed by the railway until he went to work at Keadby Power Station. Before moving to Keadby, my grandparents lived with their three children in the gatehouse on Jeffrey Lane, Belton, where my grandma operated the crossing gates. Grandma Johnson was familiar with level crossing gates as, even before she was born in 1911, her mother, Blanche Florence Emerson, was employed by the railway as their gate keeper for Low Burnham Gatehouse. My grandma lived there with her five older brothers – and, later, her two younger brothers - until 1922 when the family moved to Station Road, Epworth. Reflecting on employment as a gate keeper, it was by no means a constant grind but it must have been difficult to time the feeding, changing and comforting of babies - and Great-Grandma had eight - so that the gates were operated efficiently and thereby safely.

Robert Emerson, my great-grandfather, also worked on the railways. In 1901, he lived on Common Side Lane, Crowle, with Great-Grandma and their baby son, Thomas. Robert was employed as a railway plate layer and, on the same lane, his uncle, Young Emerson, a railway inspector, lived with his family, including his son, George, Robert's cousin, who was a railway porter. Robert was still working as a plate layer in the census of 1911 but by then was living in Low Burnham. He was building railways in France for a time in the First World War. The railway was a steady employer in the Isle of Axholme for many years but, apart from stations at Crowle and Keadby with Althorpe, there is little activity now. In my parents' wedding picture, there is one more railway connection. My Uncle Neville - William Neville Johnson - is now enjoying his retirement after a career as an engine driver, starting - as lads always did back in the day - as a fireman or engine stoker. Sometimes boys worked unpaid as engine cleaners before they were classed as firemen/stokers. It took a very long time for men to progress to driver status. It is a huge responsibility and hands-on work was considered to be of major importance with men studying in their own time while gaining the necessary experience to move upwards.

It is strange that many believe women in the workplace is a new thing. It really isn't. On the wedding photo, of the seven women, they all worked extremely hard to bring up their families and some also held down employment outwith the home. My Auntie Gwen worked as a sales assistant for Mr. and Mrs.York on Albion Hill, Epworth, sometimes taking around a suitcase full of clothes, cushion covers etc. to sell to those who requested a visit. Later on, she ran a tiny shoe shop of her own in Crowle, progressing to a larger double fronted shoe and drapery shop further up the High Street. At the same time she and my uncle, Peter Jackson, ran a small local taxi service.

My mum, June Margaret (Johnson) Temperton worked in the offices of Browns in Epworth and later in the offices of the Co-op in Scunthorpe, before leaving to bring up her family. Her sister, my Auntie Shirley (born Shirley Doreen Johnson), trained in children's nursing at Sheffield.

Granny Ivy belonged to the generation of women who would buckle up an old coat and put on a pair of wellies - not forgetting the woven headscarf - to help on the land when, for example, beet needed singling. That being done, they would go back to their regular housework with a few more pennies in the purse. Grandma Johnson, once the family had left the gate house in Belton and she no longer operated the crossing gates, worked for various employers - Simms' Florists, and Riley's Crisps of Scunthorpe, the state owned margarine factory in Keadby, Spring's canning factory in Brigg, and others, but there are two things which stand out for me. One was her job as an ice cream lady. She drove the van and sold the ices. Occasionally I would go along with her and, by then, I was old enough to realise what she was up to! She would hand over the ice creams as requested and take the money. She would also hand over ice creams to the children who didn't request them - those who stood to the side watching the others - the ones with clothes which had seen better days - and especially the children who had clearly come here from abroad. When they had taken their ice cream and wandered off with happy little faces, Grandma would take out her purse and drop a few coins into the tin. The other thing which I am grateful to be able to share is her absolute generosity with her wages. There were some things she had wished for but, once she had bought those, she spent her money on her family and friends. From my own experience, I can tell you that she provided me with the crockery and cutlery of my choice for my bottom drawer. Now that's something you don't hear much about nowadays! For centuries girls and young women had a "bottom drawer" which was set apart so that they were able to store the items they had made or collected for their eventual marriage. It was then expected that all females would marry males and they would set up home together. Before the coming of television the long winter evenings required purpose. Men and women would spend them in creative occupations such as rug making, wood carving, knitting - but rarely fine embroidery as that required a good light source and it is surprisingly recently that we have been able to work as well under electric light as in daylight. The old electric light bulbs were very dim but a whole lot better than candles, rush lights and oil lamps. Although, I have to say, it is lovely to sit in a candle-lit room and just . . . . be.

    As a child you never really know what it is that grown-ups do in order to put food on their tables. You find out about your own parents, but other people may pass you by on their bikes or on tractors or in their cars. You may notice the same person waiting at a bus stop each day. Many labourers, in the mid-twentieth century, walked to work. They appeared to wear a uniform - a flat cap, a jacket which had grown shiny with age, a pair of boots which fairly clunked when they walked along path or road and, in the winter months, an old overcoat on top of the jacket, with a mis-matched belt or binder twine drawn up around the middle. These hard-working men were to be seen on the land of the local farms doing a variety of jobs throughout the year. In the days before mechanical hedge cutters, hedging was done properly, in February, by men fully attired like this in order to keep out the cold, sometimes tying binder twine around their ankles too. The hedger's tools - the billhook, rake and mallet - enabled the gaps to be filled while thickening the hedgerow for the future. The split stems were placed to the right across the gap and poles were hammered in to support them as they grew. The hedge was topped by ethering. The whole process is a skill which, though often witnessed in my childhood days, is rarely seen now.

There are other jobs which, although not exclusive to the Isle, are very much associated with it. Warping was of huge importance to the farming economy in the Isle of Axholme, enabling land to be enhanced for the production of crops such as corn, potatoes, beans and - in earlier times - hemp and flax. The tidal river was made to work for the farmers by way of its silt deposits. In previous centuries, as now, there were those who capitalised on the success of such schemes - drainage and enclosure too. I found a reference to the Islonians' desire for acquisition of more and more land, even to the extent that they would work obsessively and live a life even more frugal and lowly than that in a poorhouse. A funny lot! Richard Popplewell, who lived in Belton, built up the largest residential estate in the Isle of Axholme in the years around 1700. When I was young, in the second half of the twentieth century, entrepreneurs were doing the same thing - changing the shapes of our larger villages as they went. Very few of us are opposed to progress - and everyone needs a roof over his/her head - but the sad part of the more recent development is the destruction of everything in the way of the developer. The 1960s provided rich pickings for demolition companies. There were jobs in building too and some local builders made a tidy sum. In the right place at the right time I suppose - but you can't take it with you!

Clockwise from above:

Grandma Florence Johnson and me at Branscombe Lodge

Mum making jam in the kitchen at Branscombe Lodge. I now keep my eggs in this jam pan.

Florence Mabel Emerson, Grandma Johnson, as a teenager.

Farming the old way - Festival of the Plough 2009.

Taken from *The Epworth Bells*, 1917

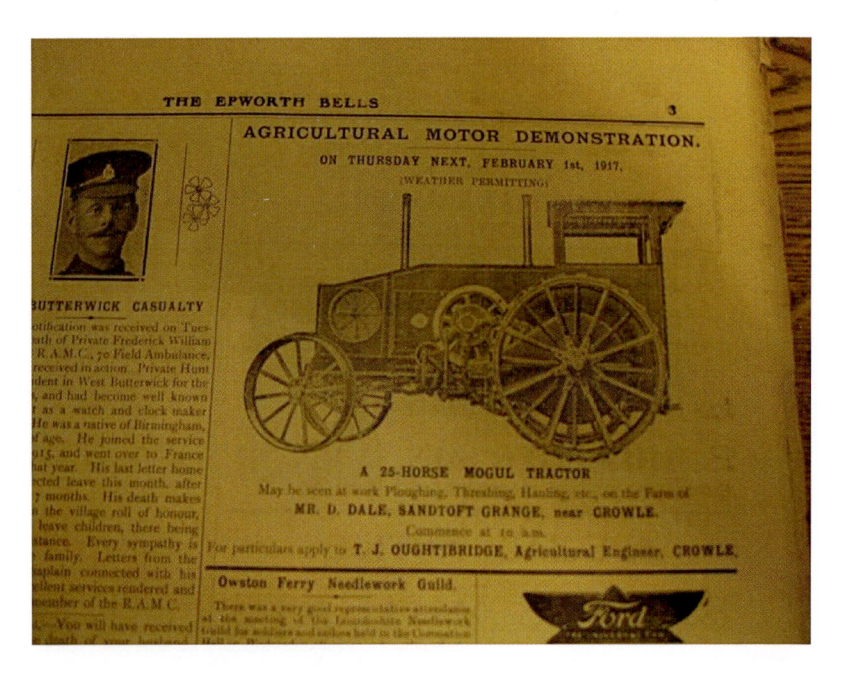

THE EPWORTH BELLS

AGRICULTURAL MOTOR DEMONSTRATION.

ON THURSDAY NEXT, FEBRUARY 1st, 1917,
(WEATHER PERMITTING)

A 25-HORSE MOGUL TRACTOR

May be seen at work Ploughing, Threshing, Hauling, etc., on the Farm of
MR. D. DALE, SANDTOFT GRANGE, near CROWLE.

Commence at 10 a.m.

For particulars apply to T. J. OUGHTIBRIDGE, Agricultural Engineer, CROWLE.

BUTTERWICK CASUALTY

Notification was received on Tuesday of the death of Private Frederick William Hunt, R.A.M.C., 70 Field Ambulance, received in action. Private Hunt resident in West Butterwick for the past, and had become well known as a watch and clock maker. He was a native of Birmingham, 41 of age. He joined the service of his country, and went over to France last year. His last letter home expected leave this month, after 7 months. His death makes in the village roll of honour, leave children, there being instance. Every sympathy is felt for family. Letters from the chaplain connected with his excellent services rendered and member of the R.A.M.C.

"You will have received death of your husband...

Owston Ferry Needlework Guild.

There was a very good representatives attendance at the meeting of the Lincolnshire Needlework Guild for soldiers and sailors held in the Coronation Hall...

Dad in his RAF days, 1947
Dad is seated second from the left.

Grandad William Johnson, on the left, working on the railway at Flixborough, 1930s
The first train ran on 11th May 1938

Santa comes to Rose Cottage, 1968

Boxing Day at Branscombe Lodge, 1968
Back Row: Mum, Dad, Mike, Auntie Gwen, Grandad Bobby, Uncle Pete
Front Row: Neil, Granny Ivy, Keith, Steve

The annual Candlemas service at St Oswald's Church, Luddington

Festival of the Plough, 2009

The Crowning Ceremony,
All Saints Church, Belton,
1971

Master John
Turner as
page boy

Clockwise from top left:

Auntie Gwen and Sandra in Auntie Gwen's shop, High Street, Crowle.

Granny Ivy Temperton with our daughter, Judith, at my mum's house, Wharf Road, Crowle, Summer 1990.

Dad and a very small Susan Linda, Battlegreen, Epworth.

Grandad Bobby's pipe - now cherished in Caithness, Scotland

My first trip to France, with the Prayt family Easter 1968
I'm on the right of the group

Mum's favourite part of the garden at Branscombe Lodge - she gardened this area by herself

Mike and me posing at the front of Studcross Cottage. I always loved the cheerful pansies

Granny Ivy, Grandad Bobby, Auntie Gwen and Mum at the back. Dad with Lassie and me at the front, Rose Cottage, 1954.

"Ring, Happy Bells, Across the Snow"

Under the heading, "Christmas and Food", "The Epworth Bells" on 22nd December, 1917, gave this advice to its readership:

As Christmas purchases are now in full swing, it is not too early, perhaps, to enter a word of appeal and reminder in regard to them. No one wants to destroy the season's tradition of festivity, which in these trying days may well be allowed to "do its bit" in keeping our hearts up. But all self-respecting people ought to set their faces against the tendency to turn festivity into the channels of excessive eating and drinking. This is emphatically not the time for either; indeed when we think of the perils and casualties daily incurred by our sailors in bringing us the necessaries of life, there is something positively indecent in wasting them upon merry-making or ostentation. The same thing applies to a great extent to Christmas presents. As far as possible these should be confined to articles of utility; the purchase of useless presents simply means the waste and misdirection of masses of labour and material, which ought to be devoted to the vital purposes of the country.

This was clearly remembered by my Great Aunt Olive (1897-1997) when I gave her household textiles one Christmas. She opened the present, looked suitably grateful - but not at all excited - and said, "A present's always better for being useful." This is the same Aunt Olive who once gave me a box of chocolates minus her favourite centres. She was such a character - you still get 'em! But oh how she loved us all. A long time ago I wrote a poem about her love of children. It was chosen for publication in an anthology but I was so much more thrilled by the fact that the priest (Revd David Schofield) at her funeral chose to read it to the congregation and said how wonderful it was that we were able to hear the children in the playground as we listened to it.

Worst Christmas memories? Well, the ones we can laugh about anyway! Our first Christmas as parents has to have a mention here. We decided to leave buying the Christmas tree until Christmas Eve - we thought it would be romantic and traditional - but it turned out to be a very silly idea - and we've never done it since! We traipsed around the appropriate shops in and around Doncaster, along the market and everywhere we passed, on the way home to Crowle, which might have had even a tiny scraggy tree - but there was no tree to be found. Fortunately my Auntie Gwen called to see Baby on his first Christmas Eve and we related the sad tale of the absent tree. She went home and sought out her old artificial tree for us. What a Christmas star! Also clear in my memory is the Christmas when we were expecting our fifth baby and we made presents for almost all the family at home and away. That year I knitted our third daughter a large leggy doll and wrapped it up with its arms crossed and legs up so that it made a neat parcel. Whatever was I thinking of? When our little girl opened it she screamed - it sprang from the wrapping paper like a huge spider. I'd potentially ruined Christmas morning! Thankfully daughter and doll made friends soon after that disastrous introduction - first impressions are not always reliable - and the doll was subsequently named Betsy. Betsy is even more elongated now and has provided much amusement over almost thirty years.

In those days, while living in Orkney, we made tape recordings of all of us - more of us as the years went by - singing carols and Christmas songs, reading poems, stories and passages from the Bible to send to Granny in Crowle as a pre-Christmas present. We were on a Scottish hillside with few near neighbours and we held our own family service each Christmas

Eve. It was so simple yet shared with genuine happiness and conviction.

The celebration of Christmas over my lifetime has evolved from those early years in the Isle when I was lucky enough to know the real Spirit of Christmas. As a child I was showered with love at Christmas. I don't mean presents - although I was always lucky in that way too - I mean love as in delight at another's joy. When I was a child in the Isle, my Christmasses seemed magical and so we put together little bits of my husband's Christmasses Past and my own Christmasses Past to give our children an awareness of the power of goodness at Christmas. It is true that, when grown-ups become parents themselves, they either kick against the goads and reject what they had as children or they take parts of family traditions and mould them to work for their new families. Whatever one's religious convictions, it cannot be denied that there is so much kindheartedness around at this time of the year. Of course I can remember some terrible misdeeds which have been committed and misfortunes which have occurred over the festive period but the sense of wanting to create a climate of joy for others prevails.

All of my growing-up Christmas Days were spent at my grandparents' home down Belshaw Lane, Carrhouse, Belton. I completely loved it. There was never a Christmas Day which did not exceed expectation. Granny Ivy worked so very hard and delighted us all. Those days, for me, are sacred to her memory. Grandad Bobby used to tell us about his Christmas stocking with such elation that he almost became a little boy again. In his stocking there would be an orange in the toe, some nuts and an apple, a few sweets and a toy. One toy. And it fitted into a stocking. So it wasn't a train set or a remote controlled boat or even an Xbox! It may have been a wooden cup with a ball on a string or perhaps a tin soldier. Instead of "sweets" Grandad called any sugary delectation, "spice". For as long as I can remember, he loved his mint humbugs and Sharps' Extra Strong Mints. I know how he made his boiled sweets last but I wonder how he ate the orange from his stocking. I love the passage in "Cranford" where Elizabeth Gaskell describes the dilemma of the ladies who were enjoying their oranges but did not want to eat them publicly. Was there a proper way for children to eat oranges? We once lived next door to a lovely Kashmiri Muslim family - we are still in touch - thank you Facebook! We have never had better neighbours. They showed our children how they ate their oranges - quartered and sprinkled lightly with salt - delicious. In their stockings our own children have always received an orange too - of the Terry's chocolate variety. They still do - and the youngest is now a teacher.

Mike and I didn't have stockings. Instead, we had a pillow case each - with large and small presents all in there together. My husband had a stocking and, when our kids were little, he loved to tell the tale of how his sister, after a naughty Christmas Eve, woke up to find coal in her stocking on Christmas morning. Our grown-up children (the ones who are with us for Christmas) still hang up the same stockings they did through their childhood Christmasses - Daddy's old walking socks. I have mended them and re-attached their hanging loops countless times but the children really don't want up-to-date replacements.

Childhood Christmasses for me were full of love - love for the Baby in Bethlehem, love for each other and love for the season itself. Michael and I would open our presents at home on Christmas morning and then we would go over to Granny and Grandad's to spend Chirstmas Day with all the family - Auntie Gwen, Uncle Peter, Steven, Keith and Neil. I couldn't wait to step through the door. The smells were wonderful. The welcome was pure joy. The Greatest Gift was not lost on us. We were full of seasonal happiness. Granny Ivy was a first rate cook and Christmas dinner was perfection. Granny cooked the dinner in the oven attached to the fireplace in the living room and also in her small electric oven in the scullery with the pudding steaming away on the hob. When I remember those dinners I think of "There never was such a goose!" from "A Christmas Carol" by Dickens and of Grandad plunging the carving knife into the breast of the turkey, sometimes a capon, sometimes a goose, just as Mrs. Cratchit had done with the Cratchits' goose. In the afternoon we children were allowed raisin wine and the grown-ups had port or sherry - but not in Bob Cratchit's "custard-cup without a handle". Before we left home my parents had slecked down our fire - the only source of heating for us in those days - with small coal and coal dust. Dad would leave the party for a while to go back and tend to the fire - and pop into the pub for a snifter!

It is interesting to think that few people had central heating in those days. Keeping warm at Christmas was tricky with some winters worse than others. At Christmastime 1962 the temperature dropped considerably. There was also fog that year and the cold weather had knock-on effects for people living in the Isle. There was an outbreak of measles and Epworth was particularly badly affected. On Christmas night 1962, Miss Nellie Temperton who lived, and taught music, on Burnham Road, Epworth, had a narrow escape when her hearth rug caught fire. Frank Lindley had noticed it as he was passing, woke up Nellie and helped her to put out the fire. Another Christmas star! I remember that as a bitter winter. It isn't the snowmen and snowball fights I remember so much as hard ground with stretches of ice everywhere and air so cold it gripped you. One hundred years ago, on Christmas Eve, there was a slight thaw, "but by midnight the wind had veered round to the north and the frost returned. Christmas Day was dry and cold, snow began to fall in the evening and on Wednesday (Boxing Day) the ground was covered, the country side looked quite Christmassy." (The Epworth Bells, 29th December, 1917)

I was the eldest grandchild and Neil was the youngest of us the year Father Christmas first came to Carrhouse on Christmas afternoon. Granny found herself a mask and put on Grandad's dressing gown. Poor Neil was terrified! When Granny . . er . . Father Christmas opened the sack of presents, things began to improve but Neil kept a close eye on Father Christmas throughout the proceedings. It has to be said, the mask was a bit scary!

Teatime was almost as splendid as Christmas dinner. Tea included a large pork pie, ham and cold turkey, salad, tarts, mince pies, buns and sweethearts. Mum had made a Christmas cake too - but more about Mum's Christmas cakes later. Sweethearts are something between biscuits and cakes with a generous dollop of homemade raspberry jam in the middle.

When the day was at an end, we drove home - tired but happy - and with quite a bit of the remaining turkey. Sometimes Mike and I would sit with Dad at our kitchen table and pick at the legs and wings with our fingers - very greasy. Those were memorable moments. Christmas Day had come to an end but we still had Boxing Day to look forward to. On Boxing Day, when I was little, the family often came to us. Mum made sandwiches, sausage rolls, trifle, jam tarts, lemon cheese tarts, coconut tarts, mince pies, maids of honour, iced buns, butterfly buns and chocolate buns. The centrepiece, however, was the Christmas cake. I'm no cake decorator - my cakes are limited to white snow with a few decorations on top but Mum's decorating, on the other hand, was a work of art. The cakes were made well in advance of the big day and left to mature - something I still do with my cake but each week I add brandy to mine - which makes it very grown-up! After several weeks the almond paste/marzipan was added and left for at least a week. That's the rule. Then it was time to put on the first layer of white icing. It was spread all over the cakes - I remember ours as being square and the one Mum made for Granny and Grandad as being a round one. The icing was smoothed and left to set. The icing of the cake took several days. After the flat white icing it was time to pipe white patterns on the top and sides. When that had set it was the turn of the very pale pink patterns and, when they were set, Mum piped on white and pink rosettes and placed silver dragees at their centres. It was all done with an icing bag - vertically as well as horizontally - and I remain in awe of the patience it must have taken to complete the decorating of just one of the cakes. Everyone was amazed at the results of Mum's labours. I was very proud and grew up to expect an annual work of art. Year after year Mum displayed her genius - at Studcross Cottage, at Aston House, at Branscombe Lodge and later at Eglantine. Wherever we lived, as I grew from being a little girl to a young woman, the Christmas cake was the centrepiece of the feast in our house. The uneaten cake was put away in a tin and sometimes there was still a little left for Mike's birthday at the beginning of March. Does anyone have secret family recipes anymore? My Grandma Johnson had a secret recipe for plum bread and she made batches of it each Christmas. A Lincolnshire tea table at Christmas wasn't complete without a plate of buttered plum bread. Margarine just wasn't acceptable. And there was no Flora Buttery in those days! Grandma also had a special recipe for Christmas puds. I have varied mine but mostly I've made up the recipe I took from a magazine the Christmas after we were married in 1976. I never make it quite the same two years running. The gluten free version I made last year - using gluten free breadcrumbs and gluten free flour - will never grace our table again! The next time the gluten-intolerant family member spends Christmas here, he will be having a tipsy fruit salad with his brandy butter!

Mum made a snowman out of a plastic barrel which had been used for salt at Riley's crisp factory - my Grandma Johnson worked there at one time and brought the barrel for us. Mum covered it with lots of cotton wool and made a head and a hat. It was filled each Christmas with sweets and chocolate - accessed by removing the head. This is a tradition I have kept up - although ours is a cotton-wool covered old-fashioned glass sweetie jar - glass clearly wouldn't pass Health and Safety - and it proves as popular with 21st century children as it did with mid 20th century kids.

Sometimes, over Christmas and New Year, we would visit my godparents for a celebration meal - either Auntie Gwen and Uncle Peter Jackson in Crowle or Auntie Maud and Uncle Peter Temperton in Wroot. I remember a scary drive between the drains when the weather was very wintry.

I wanted Christmas to last forever. Everyone was so happy, so warm-hearted and so generous.

One Christmas night, during a light snowfall, sufficient to cover the flagstones along the front of my grandparents' Rose Cottage, I wheeled my little doll's pushchair towards our car after a perfect day with my parents, my brother, my grandparents, my aunt, uncle and my cousins. I turned around to check that someone else was following with a torch. As I looked down I noticed the fine lines in the snow and understood that they had been made by the wheels of my doll's pushchair. I see those marks still in my mind's eye and remember the realisation of the beauty of it all. It is strange how little things become special memories.

It didn't always snow at Christmas but one time, on Christmas Eve, when I was in my mid-teens, I remember it snowing as my Uncle Peter Jackson drove me home to Belton from Crowle where I had been helping Auntie Gwen in her shoe and drapery shop. I loved being at Auntie Gwen's and especially at Christmastime. People would come into the shop for last minute gifts and you felt that you were a part of each individual's Christmas when you were able to help solve their present difficulties. I don't think men were so great at shopping back in those days. With a few you were able to have a conversation about their prospective purchases but with more than one the conversation was limited:

"Can I help you?"

"Looking for a nightdress for t'missus."

"What size would that be?"

(This was the point when Auntie Gwen was consulted as the gentleman rarely knew his wife's measurements and Auntie Gwen had a good idea of the sizes for everyone who shopped with her.)

"Well, this is in your wife's size and it's a really pretty lemon."

"Aye, that'll do!"

"We have this one in apricot, one in powder blue and this pink one is a little bit more expensive but it has a Nottingham lace panel across . . . ."

" First one 'll do!"

"The lemon one?"

"Aye."

And a purchase was made without a to-do!

Auntie Gwen always made me feel helpful - I'm sure I was sometimes less helpful than at other times but she never let me know. Christmas and Auntie Gwen. She passed away this summer after a long illness but I shall keep her memory in my Christmas celebrations - memories of childhood Christmas Days down Carrhouse at Granny and Grandad's, teenage Christmasses helping in her shop at Crowle and, later on,

Christmas Eves when my own children enjoyed her loving hospitality. We weren't allowed into her house though - until we had sung carols at the door - and they always had to include "Away In A Manger".

Every so often something else comes to mind for sharing and, as I was looking into the fruit bowl and reflecting on the current quality of oranges, I remembered those pre-Christmasses over half a century ago when Dad would take us to Sprakes' in Thorne to get tangerines - because in our family, in those days, all tiny oranges were called tangerines - and big juicy and sweet oranges too. We also bought various kinds of nuts, dates and red apples which were so shiny you could see reflections in them. We were still eating stored apples - and, to be honest, they probably had more taste, but the shiny ones were so attractive. Dad bought the fruit in boxes and each individual piece was wrapped in tissue paper. He sometimes bought holly and mistletoe. It was cold in the warehouse but we were mostly oblivious to the temperature. Dad was generous to a fault and shared this bounty with extended family and work colleagues alike. At our house there was no shortage of cigars, presentation boxes of cigarettes and bottles of whisky and liqueurs as the people with whom Dad had dealt throughout the year would send or deliver gifts such as these at Christmas.

England's postal service, then run by the GPO, stopped delivering mail on Christmas Day in 1960. Christmas Day deliveries went on for longer in Scotland. In "The Epworth Bells", 22nd December, 1917, Christmas postal arrangements are printed as follows:

Saturday, December 22nd, box cleared at 4.30 pm
Monday, December 24th, box cleared at 4.30 pm
Christmas Day, December 25th box cleared at 2.50 pm
Boxing Day, December 26th, box cleared at 4.45 pm
Public business on Boxing Day from 10.30 to noon.

People will be getting our cards a little later than usual this year but I hope they will arrive in advance of the big day itself! The nicest thing about being late sending out your cards is that you know the ones which plop onto the doormat at home are from the people who really want to send them! I wish we had been able to get our cards off earlier but I'm loving finding out who really wants to send us a Christmas greeting! Cards and decorations generally are more stunning now but we loved the old fashioned ones in their day. I was particularly fond of the cards which had glitter on them. This year I managed to find some of those pleated honeycomb decorations - sometimes bells, sometimes spheres - which you open out and hold in place with a paper clip. The trouble is that I didn't read the measurements carefully so we are stuck with some rather large decorations to hang from the ceiling. A bit of a fire hazard - especially as I'm so fond of candles - so I'm wondering about the wisdom of this. We had them when we were kids and we also had some very pretty Chinese lanterns which operated like a concertina and hung from the ceiling with tassels at the bottom. There were paper chains too. We sometimes made those at school. We made our own lanterns at school as well. We took a rectangle of paper and decorated it with crayons in our prettiest Christmassy patterns, then we folded it in half longways and, leaving a good edge on three sides, we cut from the fold line outwards and in evenly spaced parallel lines. We then opened out the sheet of paper, stuck the shorter edges together and attached a hanging handle. Then the base was gently pushed up and the top pushed down to create a lantern.

Lanterns conjure up an image of the waits of olden days. Do you ever wonder how our ancestors celebrated Christmas? I do. As I understand it, Oliver Cromwell et al altered Christmas well and truly, dampening the spirits of the people but not extinguishing the light. I wonder if John Temperton, whose son

William was born in West Butterwick at the beginning of the Commonwealth, clandestinely celebrated Christmas with his family. Probably a foolish thing to do in those harsh times. A reminder of past measures taken in the name of Christianity and an aid to understanding the crushing nature of al Qaeda and the Taliban in Afghanistan. Perhaps our subjugated ancestors brought in a little greenery - holly, ivy and mistletoe - or was that disallowed too? Certainly by the time his namesake, my great-great-grandfather, was born in Belton in 1829/30 there would be natural cheerful green trimmings in the cottage over the twelve days of Christmas at least. There may even have been a kissing bough which would have been made from ash or willow - plenty of both in the Isle - and then completely covered with evergreens. I think I would have gone with the ivy - especially as I well and truly punctured myself adding holly to the wreath for the front door this year. Most of it was blown off in Storm Caroline - and frankly I think it's fine without the holly!

Christmas, as a festival of light, joins Diwali, Hanukkah and others associated with various religions. The idea of fixing candles to trees was not new in the nineteenth century when Queen Victoria and Prince Albert illuminated their now very famous family Christmas tree. One idea is that Martin Luther may have been the first to light candles on an outdoor tree when he had been inspired by a starry wintry sky. They started to become popular indoors in Germany about a century after Luther and this year, as every year on Christmas Eve, our Franconian friends will bring in, decorate and illuminate with candles, their Christmas tree taken from the local forest. This year they have a baby in the family - I wish I could see his little face light up when he sees the candle-lit tree.

The electric lights we had on our tree in the fifties and sixties were large and very fragile with all manner of styles and colours all on the one string. We also had little metal candle holders, with clips to keep them on the tree, bearing cheery coloured candles. They were never lit though. We have them still - they come out year after year along with some ancient and much loved very fragile decorations. Over the years Christmas tree lights became smaller and, oddly enough, simpler. Now manufacturers offer us all sorts of lights for our trees - you can even find some which are similar to those of my childhood. Historically and geographically there are different days for taking down decorations, lights etc. and Candlemas is one such day - itself a festival of light when candles are traditionally blessed for the coming year.

Candlemas comes midway between the shortest day and the Spring Equinox. I have been to some powerful and moving services in Isle churches but, without doubt, a Candlemas service, with its procession of candles, which I attended at Luddington some years ago now was one which left an indelible sense of peace and a satisfaction that Christmas had truly completed its magic. Every year, on the Sunday closest to Candlemas, someone from nearby Waterton Hall attends Saint Oswald's in Luddington to pay 12 shillings to the priest conducting the service who would have been, centuries before, the representative of the Abbot of Selby. That part was fascinating and I went home and found out as much as I could about it. However - wonderful though knowledge is - it was the power of light in the depths of winter which spoke to me - that ongoing sense of Christmas.

Wish You Were Here

We booked our holiday for 2018 just after the year started, having done the planning between Christmas and Hogmanay. There are weekends and days away at other times, but the family holiday is set in stone. Nobody ever thought there would be no holiday this year. It is taken for granted that we will go away every year. But it wasn't always like this. I don't have to go back too far to discover a time when holidays were not the norm for my folks. There were high days and holidays in the time-off-work sense, but rarely were ordinary folk away from the family base - other than at the homes of relatives who may have moved to a different area. This would perhaps be to assist around the time of the birth of a new family member, to help with the harvest, or for some other practical reason.

Sometimes young women and girls who found themselves pregnant may have been removed to a far-away relative for a time to save embarrassment. In our tree we have more than one young woman who, in the late nineteenth century, when prudishness ruled in rural communities, left the home village and went to stay, for a while, with relations at some distance. Again, in the course of my family tree research, I have looked at many censuses and found the label "visitor" next to the names of people living under the roof with the "head" of the household at the time of the data collection. It is easy to imagine that the visitor was staying there on holiday but, on closer inspection, one may notice a new baby and/or an absent parent. It would be reasonable then to assume that the visitor was there for help and support. Women were expected to have a lying-in period after the birth of a child and there needed to be some capable person to help with her usual chores during that period. There was no paternity leave in those days. In families where the father was away for long periods of time - perhaps at sea - a female relative would make her home with the mother to give practical help with child rearing and sometimes nursing. So, except in wealthy families, a visitor was generally a useful home help rather than someone over there to partake of the air and the scenery.

Even as recently as the 1950s/60s, when I was growing up in the Isle, there were many families who did not take an annual holiday. Mum has spoken of taking a holiday with friends before she was married, but it wasn't a regular thing. It was in the first half of the 60s that we started to take family holidays. We had a holiday in Bridlington in a boarding house. It was Mum, Granny Ivy, Mike and me. Dad and Grandad Bobby went back home after spending the first day with us. We took our buckets and spades, and the ice cream money which relatives and neighbours had given to us. Grandad referred to that holiday with a twinkle in his eye as he often reminded me that I went home with more pocket-money than when I started out and he thought that was really funny. People were just so generous - and I was so careful.

We had relations in Bridlington. Granny Ivy's older sister, Auntie Dora, married Arthur Gilmour in 1914. Arthur was a fisherman and came from a Bridlington family of mariners and fishermen. Their daughter, also Ivy (born 1915), ran a guest house there when I was small. Our family - on Granny's side - was connected with the area as Granny's great-grandfather, Norton Richardson, had worked as chief boatman in the coastguard service at Ulrome, around 1851. Before that, he had followed the east coast up from Suffolk to Flamborough where he, along with four other men, ran the coastguard in the 1840s. Subsequent family links were made in the area by the Richardsons, although Norton himself returned to his native Aldeburgh, Suffolk, and died there on 1st June 1874, aged 77.

If coastal Suffolk is your thing you can stay in Magenta Cottage where Norton was living in the 1871 census.

Bridlington was a popular destination for village outings - day trips. Dear Granny Ivy - when she went on a coach trip she always felt quite poorly. She had to take her "Sealegs" to combat travel sickness. I was never a great coach traveller either, until I had to take the bus to school every day - after seven years you get a bit better! Granny loved to see and smell the sea for the first time on an outing. I thought she was a mermaid. The drive from Belton to Bridlington takes you through some pleasant scenery, and I always thought that Bridlington came rather abruptly at the end of it. The beach was good. There is the north beach and the south beach, and both are considered to be clean and family friendly. I remember tucking my skirt into my knickers so that I might paddle in the sea - still managed to get wet though! I think my grandparents enjoyed those trips to the seaside as much as we children did - Grandad with his trousers rolled up to the knees and a sunhat made from a handkerchief, and Granny having carefully and secretly removed her stockings and wearing a pair of white framed sunglasses with vivid blue lenses. Mum had an old Brownie camera for years, and this way she recorded our outings more than adequately. Dad and I shared a taste for whelks, cockles and prawns and were regular customers at the seafood stall. Sometimes Dad would take a crab home with him. If it was one which had not been dressed (prepared for eating), he would ask Granny to do it as she had learned at a young age how it was done safely. It is essential to move the gills - known as dead man's fingers - when dressing the crab. The jury is out on whether or not they will make you very ill but they are difficult, if not impossible, to digest. Granny really didn't like doing it, but she never refused. Of course, when we were at the seaside we liked to eat fried fish and chips too. It was widely accepted that nobody produced fish and chips like the fish and chip sellers at the seaside. Dad loved his food and I am pleased to report that I have inherited his appreciation of food quality. Good quality doesn't necessarily mean high prices. It seems restaurants believe sticking a whopping price label to a dish will make it more appealing – well, it may to a certain clientele, but to real food lovers it can be a joke! I also think that the way to enjoy the best food is to choose it, prepare it and cook it oneself so that the ingredients don't have time to deteriorate. This will never put restaurants out of business though, as we all need a break from the kitchen once in a while.

Bridlington and Scarborough were both considered the go-to places for seafood. When we saw the sea we would all strike up with "Oh I do like to be beside the seaside/ Oh I do like to be beside the sea/ I do like to stroll along the prom prom prom/ Where the brass band plays tiddly om pom pom . . . ." For inland lowlanders, the view of the wide sea was truly impressive. I remember feeling very perplexed as a child when we had arrived at the seaside and then, after delighting at the vast expanse of water, we had to park some distance away so that it seemed forever before we were able get down to the business of making sand castles and digging moats. The gulls were on every roof top laughing at us as we walked - far too slowly in the opinion of a little girl carrying her bucket and spade - from the car to the beach.

When I was a little older, we went to Devon, by way of Stratford on Avon, for our annual holidays and stayed in a lovely big guest house, "Swallowcliffe", in well kept grounds close to the sea at Seaton. The place is on Old Beer Road and is now a residential care home. It was tasteful, comfortable and clean, but I could never understand why Dad didn't complain about the potatoes - they were never as good as Mum's or Granny's - they'd had almost all of the goodness and flavour boiled out of them. They were sprinkled with chopped parsley, which looks very pretty but didn't improve them. Sometimes, before breakfast, Dad and I would go for a walk in Seaton and stop at a tiny cafe where Dad had a cup of tea and I had a mug of Horlicks. While we were on holiday, we visited all the local landmarks and the pretty villages, and sometimes went farther afield. My parents both loved Branscombe. Just up from the beach there was a thatched gazebo where we bought slices of sweet melon and sometimes ice cream. It was while holidaying in Devon that Mum decided on the stonework for Branscombe Lodge. She had seen houses built of a yellowish stone and decided to replicate that in Belton. It was quite unusual and so were the green tiles she chose for the roof. Goodness me, for a lady who doesn't like the limelight, poor Mum was really at centre stage over that one! It even made the front page of one of the daily nationals! The planning department had a problem with the colour - although Mum and Dad thought green tiles - especially when they had weathered a little - would blend nicely with the countryside. Eventually the green tiles were accepted - and it didn't seem unusual for other bungalows to have green tiles soon after that.

Holidays in Devon were a good fit for us. There was something to suit each of us. There were rides down pretty country lanes, substantial houses and gardens to visit, delightful beaches, and strawberry cream teas! Grandad Bobby loved his scrumpy, we took home the local butter and clotted cream, and Mum spotted plants and shrubs which she attempted to grow in our garden, firstly in Epworth and then in Belton. The snowball tree (Viburnum Opulus) was one such and, although the berries are lovely later in the year, the white balls of flowers are significant in late spring and early summer - the Tempertons' holiday time - between washing and packing potatoes and carrots and pulling peas and beans. I wonder if the variety of plants grown in these British islands has significantly increased due to the many holidays being taken abroad. Ah, go on - most of us have accepted foreign seeds or plants from friends who really shouldn't have put them in their homeward-bound luggage! And, even if we haven't, some of us have admired things growing either overseas or in another corner of Britain and found a supplier closer to home. Travel not only broadens the mind but also enriches all aspects of our daily lives.

As well as our holidays away, we also had shorter holidays in our little home from home. Our first residential caravan was at Reighton Gap between Flamborough and Filey. It was comfortable but not luxurious. Dad upgraded to a better model in Hornsea. This one had running water and electricity - and a bathroom. No more trudging to the toilet block! Mum made a little garden there - she just couldn't help herself - the soil wasn't great but she made it work for her. En route to the caravan we stopped, often for lunch, in Beverley. It is a charming minster town and, although I have only passed through it in recent years on genealogy jaunts, back in the days of our Hornsea holidays it had some really nice little shops. On one visit, after I had done quite well in exams at school, Dad bought me a beautiful fountain pen from a tiny olde worlde shop which sold only pens and writing implements. I have it still. Once we had arrived at the caravan in Hornsea, we would shop with the local grocer and, when Dad did the shopping, we went home with some unusual items - including foreign food - which Mum wouldn't touch *because* it was foreign food. I still remember the Swedish mayonnaise which came in a tube - as toothpaste does. It was really very good.

Mike took his pocket money and blew it all the first day - riding on the go-karts. Hornsea has the biggest lake in Yorkshire and quite an interesting history going back a long way, but it was not the sort of place for teenagers to hang out. I did, however, enjoy the family rides around the area with Dad, passing through the small villages, and I now wonder if he knew how closely linked those places are with his family tree. His Auntie Madge was born in Ulrome, his Auntie Dora's birth was registered in Bridlington, his Great Aunt Rebecca was registered in Scarborough, his great-grandmother died in Ulrome, his great-uncle died in Bridlington and his great-grandfather was a lifeboat man at Flamborough and Ulrome. This is just a sample of our links with the East and North Ridings of Yorkshire - there are even more further inland, especially amongst the Wolds villages: Hutton Cranswick, Bainton and North Dalton, Kirkburn and Londesborough. The seaside places were flanked by charming hamlets and villages which, in the days we stayed in Hornsea, had developed very little at all. Sometimes we would stay until Monday morning - Dad didn't waste any time getting from Hornsea to Belton. We clocked up some frightening speeds but I don't remember ever being afraid with Dad. He was a superb driver - even if he may have occasionally broken the speed limit. Not good though - especially nowadays with so much more traffic and many more distractions around. Dad had trained as a driver in the R.A.F. as well as driving buses, lorries and taxis closer to home. He knew a well-built vehicle and his ambition to own a Jaguar was first realised when we lived at Aston House. After that he regularly changed his car - for another Jaguar!

Across the other side of the country, Blackpool was well worth a visit at the time of the illuminations. Today most towns are well lit for Christmas but, in the 60s, the type of display created for the Blackpool Illuminations was something seen only rarely. For children - but not exclusively for children - each autumn offered a tram ride of excitement, colour and expectation. The lights never seemed to end. One brilliant spectacle after another. We stayed in Blackpool with Grandma and Grandad Johnson and had some wonderful times there. They liked to watch a show in the evening and there were some famous artists who appeared in Blackpool - names like Arthur Askey, Norman Wisdom, and Tessie O'Shea. And, of course, there was the rock. It was essential to take home a selection of Blackpool rock for family and friends. The entertainer George Formby had quite a talent for double entendre and, with his song, "With my little stick of Blackpool rock", he had wowed the ladies years before - at the same time ensuring the sugary confection made and sold in Blackpool would evermore remain a classic. We also went to Morecambe sometimes. Apart from the potted shrimps, it is the rain which stays in my mind - however it did mean that everything planted in the parks grew successfully. Rhododendrons! The rainfall was perfect for them and, in those days, we knew little of the way they pushed out our native species so we beheld them as beauties. And they were quite magnificent in Morecambe.

We occasionally went to London too - and had a good time, Dad made sure of that - but London, for me at any rate, seems very impersonal and I wouldn't have wanted to stay for any length of time. I've been back since then, but not recently. I still felt the same - one toe in to test the water and to get a flavour of the capital - then plan the homeward journey! While in London, I've seen motor shows, splendid architecture, watched classic plays and musical extravaganzas in first class theatres and visited world famous museums - as well as some lesser known ones - but I always felt the masonry pressing in around and over me.

My first trip abroad was with school on an exchange visit to Montélimar in Provence. My host family, living on the edge of a village which someone thought would match Belton, were very warm and welcoming. They did not, however, provide me with the facilities required for an exchange pupil and the community was as unlike the one I had left behind as it was possible for a rural community to be. I was offered free transport home but I declined the offer and have never regretted it. My experience gave me an insight into the lives of subsistence-living Europeans - probably equating to conditions in the late-eighteenth/early-nineteenth centuries. You just don't forget something like that - and you learn much about humanity from it. The second exchange visit was guaranteed to be completely different. I was put with a wealthy family, again very welcoming, but the elegant house, and the space and freedom made me a little inclined to loneliness. There were some great outings though and, with my school friends, Shirley Key and Noreen Bond (we are friends still), I learned a great deal about the culture and the geography of the area. I was disappointed to discover recently that, due to improved infrastructure in Provence, thereby diverting potential visitors away from Montélimar itself, a number of the world famous nougat factories have now had to close - though, thankfully, not all.

Wasn't it generally the case that, when we left to go on holiday, those who did not go along with us emphasised we that should "have a nice time". Our teachers were constantly telling us not to use the word "nice" in our writing because there were so many other words which would better describe what we wanted to convey. So what was a "nice" time? Was it something which could be better? Was it something which should be frowned upon? Should it be a guilty secret? A "nice" time turned out to be something completely different. Something which was a break from the daily routine. So does it follow that the daily routine was not "nice"? I don't think so - but living a little differently for a while and widening the horizon only serves to improve our regular lives and kindles interest in subjects we would perhaps otherwise never have considered. The line we wrote on our holiday postcards was maybe a bit of a fib then. If we really "wish you were here" - and the recipient actually turns up - just how much of a change would that be? Getting away is beneficial - even if it only serves to make one love home more! "A change is as good as a rest" - so those on their travels experience the change and those back home have a rest. Both good - but you can get too much of a good thing and not everyone wants to spend long periods of time away, not forgetting that holding the fort back home will not always be through choice.

After the school summer holidays we returned to school, the smell of fresh paint, and new coat pegs. We had grown in more than stature - our summertime experiences, whether at home or away, had built on our confidence and we were raring to go. Such are the benefits of taking a break, and long may it remain possible for us to do so.

On The Street Where You Live

Imagining your home with other people living in it, at a time before you moved in, is quite fun yet also a little bit sad. Sad because something made them move away. It may have been a job or perhaps the family grew up - or it may have been too hard to continue living there after the loss of a family member - or some other reason entirely. The house itself is inanimate but, to you, it wraps its walls around your family, keeping them sheltered and safe.

The house we live in now is a part of Thomas Telford's plan for Pulteneytown, south of the River Wick. There are houses around the harbour, originally intended for those working with the herring, and houses further up the hill, some of which, like ours, were built for the managers and bankers etc.. Now, though, our square is just outside one of the most deprived areas of the Scottish Highlands. At the time of construction, around 1840, it would have been a wee bit glam. When we moved to this house we set about giving it back its character - leaving the central heating and double glazing. Most prefer the trend for simple lines and there is nothing pared back about Victorian design, but we are comfortable with the shapes in relief on the walls where a lintel remains or where the arc of a fireplace acts as a reminder that bedrooms were heated even back then! We are excited by the history of it and have done research which informs us of early decor and previous occupants and how the garden was laid out, who the neighbours were - even where some of the people, who had lived here, moved on to. I am simply unable to dismiss the past and it is my belief that a remembrance is a prayer.

Having flitted many times, I've never forgotten the people who lived close by me. Writing this series of memories has been a privilege in that I have been able to renew my acquaintance with those who helped shape this Child of the Isle. Many have died, but that does not stop me remembering them and being thankful for their smiles, their ways and their many kindnesses. Even those who showed me no kindness at all had a valuable part to play. The odd thing is that I don't recall many unkind people - one or two, maybe a few more over a lifetime - but my family smile fondly at me when I show no glimmer of recollecting a slight or provocation. Negativity slips so easily into nothingness. At the bottom of my heart there is true gratitude for each one of those Axholme folk who contributed to the development of this peculiar human being.

I remember those who lived around my first home on Belshaw Lane, Carrhouse, Belton. I can't remember them from the time I was living there up to being six months old, but they were still there during my early years so I have memories of them from visiting my grandparents and, later, from my teenage years when we were living at Branscombe Lodge at the other end of the road. We were living diagonally across from Granny Ivy and Grandad Bobby in the first few months of my life and, next to them, on their west side, was a secluded garden in the middle of which stood a rather gloomy house. The size and shape of the house were quite pleasing but the surrounding darkness gave an eerie feel to the whole. In that house, rarely seen, lived Jack Needham, brother of Fred who lived at his other side on Northferry Lane. Mr and Mrs Ralph Hackney lived at the corner of Belshaw Lane and Northferry Lane with their family - Stephen, Sheridan, Michael and Christine - and at the bottom of Northferry Lane lived the Beecrofts - Mr and Mrs Beecroft, Philip, Paul and Julie.

Jack Needham was born in Bawtry and Fred, six years his junior, was born in Doncaster. Their father was a cabinet maker, originally from Epworth. When my father bought Jack's house and garden, after Jack's death, we found some beautiful examples of the craftsmanship of Mr. Needham Snr.. Jack had suffered with a nervous illness since he was a teenager and that resulted in his living the life of a recluse. His brother, Fred, on the other hand, was very much an open and welcoming man. He was married to Eva, who was the sister of Ernie Addlesee, a near neighbour of ours when we lived in Branscombe Lodge. Ernie's house, across the road from Crosshill Farm where Mrs. Franks lived and which is now owned by the Glews, was a man-stop where the local grapevine started off the process of fermentation. I remember the gents leaning against the wall, looking outward so that anything which may be occurring was not missed. Some would pull up their bicycles and just stop for a few minutes - not for as long as the others. The congregation of Ernie's visitors was a work of art to me - and a bit of an eye-opener! I mean *really*, in those days we were told that it was the ladies who liked to natter. Ernie must have been the go-to person in Belton if one needed information - even though he lived on the edge of the village.

People came and went, but the inhabitants of Carrhouse stayed mostly the same. The little lanes and verges were so familiar they may have been the veins on the back of my hands. Delivering the church magazine with Granny gave me the opportunity to visit those local people who did not often venture from their own plots. In those days, there were quite a number of people who stayed put and really didn't feel the need to travel. Mr and Mrs Walt Kitson were our neighbours too and, in the tiny lane behind them, Mrs Annie Burgess lived alone after the death of her husband. Another lane ran in front of Granny and Grandad, and that is where Mr and Mrs Sam Fox lived. Further along was the home of Mr and Mrs John Wall. Mr Wall was a special constable - one of the noble band of volunteers who were ready for emergencies. I'm unsure whether policing the traffic flow at Epworth and District Agricultural Show was their reason for joining, but it is always nice to see familiar faces moving through the fair wearing a reassuring uniform.

When I was small, Great-Auntie Rose lived in a little bungalow down Carrhouse. She was married to Billy Clark and died, in February1965, when I was eleven and before we moved back to live down Carrhouse. Auntie Rose was Grandad Bobby's sister and she and Uncle Billy built their bungalow on Temperton land halfway along the road, on what is now known as Belshaw Lane. (Belshaw Lane used to be Bellshaw Lane and started at the Carrhouse junction with Northferry Lane, going through to the Epworth/Sandtoft road.) After starting off his business with Walter Law in Church Street, Epworth, Dad moved his carrot washing plant to the plot next to Auntie Rose. There was a large pit of slurry behind the carrot-washing shed. It smelt absolutely foul. We've all allowed a carrot to rot amongst our vegetables at one time - multiply the intensity of the noxious aroma by a significant figure and you are part way to understanding how awful it was.

When Dad no longer washed carrots, Don Armitage used the carrot shed as a garage and, for a while, my brother, Mike, helped there. Judges, the hauliers, kept lorries on the site at one time. Auntie Rose and Uncle Billy lived next to a small group of willows, an indicator that here, once upon a time, there was marsh. The marsh has mostly gone now but there remains, in places, a legacy of native trees and plants for the keen eye to observe. Eastwards, between their bungalow and Devon House, the home of Mr.and Mrs. Goodlad, was a strip of a field. Mr. Goodlad sold greengroceries from a large van. I remember it rolling into his entrance with as much stability as the wagons in the wild west. There was a small orchard at the other side of Devon House and then a strip of ploughed land before reaching

Ernie Addlesee's house on the corner. On the other side of the road there were fields between my grandparents and Crosshill Farm.

Going back now to when I was a baby - after moving from Carrhouse to Epworth, Mum and Dad first lived in Battlegreen. It was the sleepiest triangle of Epworth - belying its label - with several working farms. The house faced into the yard which was shared with the Moore family - Archie and Maud Moore, their sons, Russ, Gordon, Doug and their daughter, Monica. The family was in the building trade. When I was at school Mr. and Mrs. Moore's grandaughter, June Drinkall, was there at the same time but was a couple of years older than me. June's mum was Gwen, the older daughter of Mr. and Mrs. Moore. The Drinkalls lived a stone's throw from Battlegreen, on Coronation Crescent. Pedestrian access to Coronation Crescent was across the road from Epworth County Primary School. There was a small area of sand at the entrance and you knew it was summer when small children took their Matchbox vehicles and excavated there. The girls used the low railing as gym apparatus and timid wildflowers like birdseye and daisies attempted to recolonise the rough grass left behind after the post-war builders. But we are over on the other side of Battlegreen now and we need to journey past the back entrance to the Thurlow Playing Field (the front entrance being on Station Road)and turn to the right to return to the area where we lived in 1954.

On the corner of Battlegreen and Station Road was the home of Mr and Mrs George Tune. Dad worked for Mr Tune before working for George Lindley on Greengate. I have an image of iron railings around an elegant double fronted house. To the Battlegreen side were the buildings used for storing potatoes etc.. There was space in front of these for turning trucks and lorries. In another garden on the same side of the road was a monkey puzzle tree (Chilean Pine). All children loved monkey puzzle trees in those days. We had little experience of such exotic plants and the ones which grew to maturity in English villages became local legends. I heard recently that these trees are now under threat in their native Chile. As they can live for one thousand years it is possible that the puzzle for the little monkeys of Battlegreen is flourishing there still.

When we moved on to Studcross Cottage our address was still Battlegreen, so Studcross is a part of Battlegreen. Where Battlegreen turned sharp right to go to Wroot there was the option to go straight ahead where the road became a dusty track in summer, a quagmire in autumn and a series of knife-like ridges in icy winters. Just before the corner Pat Coggan lived with her parents and her teddy bear, Sammy. They kept pigs in clean and roomy outhouses. When a new litter had been born, the overall sound coming from the yard went up several octaves. There is something so characterful about a piglet - bald and in the pink with an insatiable curiosity. They never seem noisy on their own - it is when the whole family strikes up that one feels the need for ear plugs.

Moving "up street" to Aston House meant new neighbours and a very different view. Instead of fields our view was of the street and of people walking, biking and driving past. Across the road lived the Selby families, next door to each other in a pair of elegant semis. John lived with his parents on the left and Stephen lived with his parents on the right. To the right of Stephen was the HORSA site. HORSA stands for "Hutting Operation for the Raising of the School Leaving Age". This hut building went on when the school leaving age was raised to fifteen in 1944. That part of Epworth High Street was quite leafy and we also had trees behind us in and around our back garden. When I was at school at the HORSA site - it was used for primary education too - Mr. Percy Lindley, who lived in a red brick bungalow on the other side of the site, gave acorns to us with instructions on how to plant them. I duly planted mine at Studcross Cottage. I wonder - is there an oak tree in the garden there?

Traffic was not going at speed when it passed our house as we were close to the traffic lights. There was nothing like the number of cars then - in fact there were so few that Mike and I had the opportunity to jump on the rubber strip which went half way across the carriageway to regulate traffic. Not always little angels then.

There had been gas to Aston House at one time, but it was sealed off when we moved in. One frightening day, however, we were able to smell gas and, as a result, the road and footpath had to be closed while the gas people made the house safe. I don't remember much about it really, so my parents must have done a good job of keeping calm. Fortunately, Tottermire Lane runs to the north of the house, so a diversion should have been relatively straightforward.

When we moved back to Carrhouse and into our bungalow on Belshaw Lane, Mrs Franks was living next door at Crosshill Farm and she kept chickens there. It was good to be in the countryside again - although Epworth was never a metropolis. I loved to watch the hares playing in the fields at the side and behind us in Belton. After many years of watching hares, I am still fascinated by the way they relate to each other and how they remind me of horses. I've seen them disappear in a meadow, box in the dust of a field margin and lollop across the snow - I never cease to be uplifted by their antics.

After our bungalow went up, the way was opened for infilling and now there are a number of properties along the road there. Mr. and Mrs. James and their children - Owen, David and Gwynneth - were our next-door-neighbours in the new houses. At the time it seemed mildly odd that they were "not from roond eer". Carrhouse still housed the descendants of people who lived there centuries before and incomers were, back in those days, a bit of a peculiarity. Mr. Harrison built the bungalows next to us. They had quite long gardens which are now well established. When Mr. Harrison was building he used to sing Italian ballads as he worked. I rather enjoyed that. He was married to an Italian lady and the twist to this bit of the story lies in the fact that she introduced me to the use of rosemary in cooking. Soon after Keith and I were married we bought the house the Harrisons had built for themselves in Crowle. With the house came a well-established rosemary bush and Mrs. Harrison explained how important it was for her to have one by the back door. We have moved six times and over hundreds of miles since then, and I still have a rosemary near to the back door.

Rosemary for remembrance.